The Believer's Call to Commitment

The Andrew Murray CHRISTIAN MATURITY Library

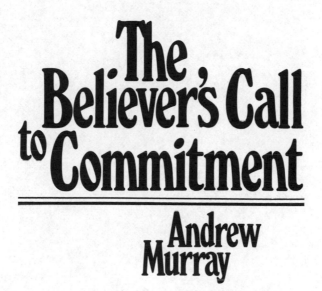

The Believer's Call to Commitment

Andrew Murray

BETHANY HOUSE PUBLISHERS
MINNEAPOLIS, MINNESOTA 55438
A Division of Bethany Fellowship, Inc.

ISBN 0-87123-289-8

Published by Bethany House Publishers
A Division of Bethany Fellowship, Inc.
6820 Auto Club Road, Minneapolis, Minnesota 55438

Printed in the United States of America

The Author

ANDREW MURRAY was born in South Africa in 1828.
After receiving his education in Scotland and Holland, he
returned to that land and spent many years there as both
pastor and missionary. He was a staunch advocate of bibli-
cal Christianity. He is best known for his many devotional
books.

Contents

Preface

Several years ago I was asked to write a series of articles under the heading, "Aids to Devotion," for the *Lovedale Christian Express.* At that time I was deep in a study of the Epistle to the Ephesians. I thought it might be possible to connect this study with the request to assist the devotional emphasis of their periodical. This led to my writing two of the introductory chapters and the twelve chapters that deal with the prominent elements of this epistle.

I am deeply aware of my inability to fully express what I think I have seen of the treasures that God has stored away in this epistle for His Church. I have, nevertheless, ventured forward in the publication of the material in the hope that God may use it to help some of His children realize two essential truths: first, the standard of the true Christian life as it is set before us in Ephesians; and, second, the divine assurance that God is able and willing to make true in our experience all that the epistle contains.

I send this book out with the prayer that Paul wrote in his epistle, "that the God of our Lord Jesus Christ, the Father of glory, may give unto you the spirit of wisdom and revelation in the knowledge of him." Without the Holy Spirit being sought, received, and yielded to in great teachableness, the truths of the epistle will remain a hidden mystery to our spirits. With a teachable spirit, we shall "be filled with the knowledge of his will in all wisdom and spiritual understanding." As spiritual men, we shall learn to know that which surpasses human knowledge and be enabled to experience His power—the power to do in us "exceeding abundantly above all that we ask or think."

Andrew Murray

Clairvaux, Wellington, S.A.,
October 26, 1909

Other Books by Andrew Murray

CHAPTER ONE

Devotional Life and Commitment

"Pray to thy Father which is in secret; and thy Father which seeth in secret shall reward thee openly" (Matt. 6:6).

We use the word "devotion" in two senses: first, with regard to prayer in our public and private devotions; and, second, with regard to the spirit of devotion, or commitment (devotedness) to God, which is to be the mark of our daily life. We have these two thoughts in our text. If in our private devotions we truly meet our Father who sees in secret, He has promised us the open reward of grace to live our life to His glory—the entire and continual commitment of our entire personality to His will. The act of commitment in private devotion secures the power for that spirit of commitment which is to extend through our daily life to His glory.

An outstanding passage concerning this principle of commitment to God is found in Lev. 27:28: "No devoted thing, that a man shall devote unto the Lord . . . shall be sold or redeemed; every devoted thing is most holy unto the Lord." The story of Achan (Josh. 6:17, 18) is a solemn

13

commentary on how this principle works out: "The city shall be accursed. . . . And ye, in any wise keep yourselves from the accursed thing, lest ye make yourself accursed, when ye take of the accursed thing and make the camp of Israel a curse." "Accursed" means devoted or committed to God for destruction. The punishment, first on Israel in its defeat and then on Achan, gave a somber illustration of the serious meaning of devotion or commitment in God's sight. Commitment is the wholehearted and irrevocable surrendering to God of what may never be taken back again. The person or thing is "most holy to the Lord."

Helping to strengthen commitment may be accomplished by many methods. The simplest method would be to offer insight concerning our time of private devotion— how to make it a time of worshiping God in truth. With this method we would deal with the chief hindrances we find to an effective devotional life and some of the reasons that these hindrances have such power over us. This method would also seek the disciplines that enable us to pray more effectively. In a book like Dr. Moule's *Secret Prayer,* one finds many helpful thoughts, supplying just what is needed in this direction. Another method would be to meditate on a series of Scriptures; thereby, encouraging desire and strengthening faith. Scriptural meditation awakens the reader's spiritual receptivity and sensitivity. His devotional life becomes a joy through the awareness that it is pleasing to God. A book, for instance, like Bowen's *Daily Meditations,* or Spurgeon's *Day Book,* has been found helpful to many.

But there is still another method which, though more difficult, has its advantages. It does not deal directly with the devotional life, but with that spirit of commitment and temper which is to rule us moment by moment, and to fill the actions or our common life with true devotion to God. The main purpose of this method would be to challenge the personal character of the believer's spiritual life. The believer would be challenged on the following points: what he truly regards as the meaning of a life wholly surrendered to God, His will, and His glory; the thought he has of the extent to which this commitment is absolutely obligatory and attainable; what he thinks of his successes or failures in the past and their causes; and, the amount of discipline and self-denial which he counts necessary to succeed in the pursuit.

Educators constantly tell us that the primary rule in all teaching is this: the mind of the pupil is to be aroused and stimulated to self-activity. It is only when you have instilled within him the awareness of his own abilities, and have helped him to realize the joy of victory over apparently insurmountable difficulties, that you really give him the key by which he can discover truths for himself. No one can do us a greater favor than by stimulating spiritual thought and desire. This spiritual stimulation will cause us to unreservedly pursue the work of training ourselves to seek with our whole heart that life of commitment which will be most pleasing to God.

Many have called Socrates the greatest teacher the world has ever seen. He was not a communicator of knowledge; he simply asked questions. He helped his scholars, first to see their own ignorance, then to know their abilities of thought and reason, and then to understand that the real value of knowledge is contained in its moral power (as the truth was received in the heart and the life). More than one humble and thoughtful inquirer owed to him the unfolding of all that was meant in his words, "Know thyself."

In these days when men profess to have little time for personal meditation on divine truth, we might well desire a modern Socrates to arouse us by his questions. Do we really understand the words we use and believe the truths we profess? The heathen Socrates might teach many believers the meaning of true religion and give them strong reason to strengthen their commitment. One of our religious writers is much like Socrates in his method of teaching—William Law. With his deep insight, he clearly depicts the lack of reality in much of traditional beliefs. He exposes the inconsistency between a faithful observance of our public or private devotions and a life committed to the world. He seeks to make us know ourselves, both in our ignorance and in the abilities that lie dormant in us. And just as Socrates always appealed to the voice within him, "that a god had ordered him to spend his life in proving to himself and others whether we are giving ourselves to right living," so Law, especially in his later writings, ever aimed to arouse the faith that Christ dwells in the heart and that despite all our ignorance and impotence, we may count upon the help of His life and Spirit.

A few words from the first chapter of Law's *Serious Call*, on the nature of Christian commitment, will illustrate this. "There is not a shadow of a reason why we should in our prayers look wholly to God, and pray according to His will, but what equally proves it necessary for us to look wholly to God, and make His will and His glory the rule of our daily life. . . . There is no reason why our prayers should be wise and holy and heavenly, but that our lives may be of the same nature, and that we may live to God in the same spirit that we pray to Him."

The first lesson is: *our lives must be as holy as our prayers.* Our prayers are tested by the fruit they bear in the holiness of our life. True commitment in prayer will be rewarded by God's grace with the power to live a life of true commitment to Him and His service. "Pray to thy Father in secret, and thy Father which seeth in secret will reward thee openly."

Let Socrates, let William Law, let our own heart and conscience enforce the questions which these thoughts suggest. Or rather, let Jesus Christ himself, our blessed teacher, guide us to find out whether our commitment is such as He asks: a full surrender to God in private every day, and a full commitment to His glory all the day.

CHAPTER TWO

Commitment—
The New Testament Standard

"Howbeit for this cause I obtained mercy, that in me first Jesus Christ might show forth all longsuffering, for a pattern to them which should hereafter believe on him to life everlasting" (1 Tim. 1:16).

In any judgment we pronounce, everything will depend upon the standard we use. Those who are content with the level of ordinary Christianity, though they may admit that their own commitment is lacking, will not be deeply convicted of its sinfulness or of the need and the possibility of any higher attainment. But, when we begin to see what the standard of the New Testament is, and its universal obligation, we see how far we come short of it. We become convicted of the great sin of unbelief in the power of Jesus to keep us from sin and to enable us to live a life pleasing to God. We find in God's Word that no matter how impossible the standard is with men, it is not impossible to the God who works in us to will and to do by the power of His Holy Spirit.

Discovering the New Testament standard of commitment is not an easy matter. Our preconceived opinions blind us; our environment will exercise a powerful influence. Unless there is a very sincere desire to truly know the entire will of God, and a prayerful dependence on the Holy Spirit's teaching, we will search in vain. Let everyone who is willing to live entirely for God and desires in everything to please Him be of good courage: God wants us to know His will and has promised by the Spirit to reveal it to us.

Paul tells us that Christ made him a pattern for all believers, and frequently admonishes the churches to follow his example (1 Cor. 4:16; 11:1; Phil. 3:17; 4:9; 1 Thess. 1:6; 2 Thess. 3:9). In studying the true type of New Testament commitment, we cannot do better than take Paul as a pattern. The question might be asked, "Why, when God had given His Son as our perfect pattern, should Paul also be needed?" The answer is of deep importance.

Many look upon Christ in His sinless perfection as so utterly beyond what we can attain that His example loses much of its force. In Paul, the chief of sinners, we feel that here is a man of like passions and desires with ourselves. In him Christ gave proof, for all time, of what He could do for a sinner in saving and keeping from sin.

What Christ has done for him, He can and will do for us, too. If we Christians would only make a careful study of the life of commitment which Christ enabled Paul to live, we would be one step nearer the time when absolute and entire commitment to God, as set before us in Scripture, would be counted essential to a true Christian life.

Someone may ask, "How can there be such a difference between the standard in our churches and that of the New Testament? Do not our creeds give God's Word the place of honor, and acknowledge Scripture as our only guide?" A little reflection will suggest the answer. Not long after the first generations of Christians had passed away, terrible corruption entered into the Church. In the course of time the Church sank into the darkness of the Middle Ages. With the Reformation and the preaching of "justification by faith," there was a great revival of Christian truth, but without the corresponding revival of Christian life and practice.

When the Bohemian Brethren, followers of John Huss, whose church order for the spiritual care of their members proved how doctrine and life were indissolubly linked together, sent deputations to the Reformers, Calvin congratulated them that, in addition to pure doctrine, they maintained such good discipline and morals. He adds, "We have long since recognized the value of such a system, but cannot in any way attain to it." Brucer, another Reformer, wrote, "You alone in the whole world combine a wholesome discipline with pure faith. When we compare our church with yours, we must be ashamed."

While we bless God for the Reformation, we must never forget that *it was not Pentecost*. The spirit and power of Pentecost was something infinitely greater. Church history tells us that it took a half a century or more before some of the great doctrines of our creed were fully understood and formulated. It was not given to any generation to develop more than one truth at a time.

This was also true during the Reformation. All the strength of the Reformers was needed to free the great doctrine of "justification by faith" from the errors under which it had been buried. The full exposition of the doctrines of sanctification, the power and work of the Holy Spirit, and the calling of the Church to preach the Gospel to the lost were left to later generations.

Even now in studying a momentous question like the true standard of spiritual commitment to God, we must beware of looking to the Reformation or later ages for our answer. Our only security is in the careful study of what Pentecost and the Scriptures set before us. If God through the revelation of His Son in Paul gave him as an example and a guarantee of what He could do for us, we may be sure that Paul's example of commitment, self-sacrifice, joy and victory will help us to find the path in which we can live well-pleasing to God.

I do not know how to plead with sufficient earnestness to stimulate God's children to make their private devotions a means of cultivating *clearer insight into what God is absolutely willing to do for us.* There is a life prepared by God himself waiting to be revealed in us by the Holy Spirit if we are only ready to realize and confess how much there is lacking in our spiritual life.

Let us take two simple truths in regard to the Holy Spirit as our guide. The one, that the Church of today is characterized by feeble workings of the Holy Spirit. The other, that God's Word has promised the mighty working of God's Spirit in the hearts of His children. If we accept the first of these truths, we take our place in penitent confession of how little we have honored the Holy Spirit and how little we have lived up to what He is willing to work in us. In confession we will find our hearts drawn to a new and larger faith in the mighty workings of the Spirit which God has promised. Our private devotions each day will far eclipse the human standard we have been content with, and an ever-widening entrance into a life in the Spirit, which God has provided, will assuredly be revealed to us.

As we pursue our study, let us fix our attention on three simple questions: (1) Does Scripture lay down a standard of attainment for those who wholly surrender themselves to the Spirit and trust in God's almighty power to work in them what He asks? (2) Is it true that the Church as a whole does not live up to the standard that God has actually made possible to attain? (3) Are we ready to yield ourselves with our whole heart to accept what God has prepared?

CHAPTER THREE

Commitment—
The Great Need of the Church

"Because ye are sons, God hath sent forth the Spirit of
his Son into your hearts, crying, Abba, Father" (Gal. 4:6).

When God had revealed His love in the gift of His Son,
His great work was completed. When Christ had died upon
the cross, with His "It is finished," and had been raised up
and seated upon the throne of God, His work was completed. Then began the dispensation of the Spirit, whose office
it was to reveal and impart all that the work of God and of
Christ had prepared. This work of the Holy Spirit has not
yet been accomplished; it is for this that Christ sits upon
the throne until all His enemies are made His footstool.

There is a great difference between the work of the
Father and the Son, and of the work of the Holy Spirit. The
Father and the Son accomplished their work for and on the
behalf of men, as a salvation prepared for their acceptance.
The Holy Spirit's work is to impart to men that grace which
enables them to accept and to live out what the Father and
the Son have provided. The distinguishing mark of the
operation of the Spirit is that His work and man's work are

21

inextricably linked together, so that whatever the Spirit does He does through man, and whatever is to be done in the kingdom of God is accomplished by man. In the world of men, the Holy Spirit can manifest himself only in, and as, the spirit of man. The work of the Holy Spirit emphasizes the dynamic role of man in the carrying out of God's plan.

When Paul had spoken of God in Christ reconciling the world to himself, he immediately adds, "He hath committed unto us the word of reconciliation." The carrying out and making known of the reconciliation was entrusted to the Church. Upon the Church's faithfulness or failure would depend the spread and the power with which that reconciliation would work in the world.

These thoughts suggest to us the wonderful glory of the work of the Holy Spirit, the terrible failure on the part of the Church, and the only path to restoration.

God's great reason for sending the Spirit of Christ to take possession of the hearts of men was to restore the fellowship with himself for which man had been created. All the work of God and of Christ in redemption culminated in this one thing—the Holy Spirit was to communicate the salvation that had been provided and to maintain it in unbroken effectiveness, moment by moment, in the hearts of God's children.

He was to be the Spirit of life, leading believers in the path of holiness and perfect conformity to Jesus Christ. He was to be the Spirit of power, equipping them for service, as Christ's witnesses, to the ends of the earth. The Holy Spirit was to be the perfect bond of union between the Father in heaven and the believer on earth. The bond of union, too, between Christ and the perishing world. Every believer would, in the power of the Spirit, be able to communicate his testimony concerning the love that had come to him. God's great purpose was that man should be saved not only in Christ His Son, but through the men in whom He lived. The gift of the Spirit rendered this possible and certain in everyone who surrendered himself absolutely to be indwelt by Him.

How miserably the Church has failed in its high calling. How few there have been, like Paul, who have proven that absolute dependence upon the Holy Spirit does secure the continual presence and working of God in daily life. Is not the distinctive mark of the Church the feeble workings of the Spirit of God? Is not the reason that there is so much prayer for the power of the Holy Spirit, with so little results, because so few are ready to yield themselves absolutely to His control? They do not know the one secret of coming under the fullness of His power—that unceasing dependence upon the work of the Holy Spirit will result in death to the self-life and a counting upon God to do His perfect work. It is when the Church, when the believer, begins to understand this that there will be a hope for the true revival of the Spirit in divine power.

Thank God for the assurance that the Holy Spirit has been given, that He is yearning over us, that He is ready and able to indwell His Church. Let us be ready to honestly confess the true condition of the Church and the responsibility we have in it. Let all who believe in God, in His love and His almighty power, bear their testimony to the one thing needful and the one thing above everything most certain—*that God is longing to enter in the power of the Spirit into possession of His redeemed people.* Let us lift our voices heavenward, to plead in unceasing intercession that God would manifest himself to all who are longing to be temples of the Holy Spirit. May our one desire be that of being filled with His power, yielded completely to be made suitable for the dwelling, the worship, the service of the living God.

And what is the connection between what we have said and the commitment of daily life? Nothing less than this: our aim in our private devotions must ever be to cast aside the accepted standard of religion and to make God's standard the object of our unceasing desire. God's Spirit has been given to reveal Christ and His life in us. No true spiritual progress can be made until with purpose of heart we determine that in everything we shall live in immediate and unceasing dependence upon the power of the Holy Spirit.

I have already suggested what will be some of the great hindrances. We may not have understood His claim to have absolute and entire control. We may lack faith and trust in His gracious and tender love to meet us and work His work of power in our hearts. We may be ignorant of the power of the world as the great enemy of the blessed Spirit. We may be unwilling to take up the cross of Christ, to die with Him in His death as the Spirit alone can reveal it. Or, to summarize these hindrances, there may be *the absence of that deep conviction of what a holy, divine, and almighty work it is for God the Spirit to take possession of our life and to carry out His one desire to make Christ live within us.*

God help us to remember that it is in our daily commitment to Him that this great work is to be carried on and accomplished. God help us to be strong in faith, giving glory to God, trusting in His ability to give life to the dead and to carry out His own work in us. We cannot overemphasize the thought that the one great reason God gave the gift of the Holy Spirit was to equip His people for *being* and *doing* what they could not be and do in the Old Testament. God does not expect from us, however earnest our efforts and our prayers may be, that we should strengthen and maintain our own spiritual life. That is the work for which His Holy Spirit was promised. It is only the soul who lives in entire surrender to and dependence on the blessed Spirit in whom God can effectually carry on His mighty work and accomplish all His blessed purposes.

CHAPTER FOUR

Commitment and the Spiritual Life

"Blessed be the God and Father of our Lord Jesus Christ, who hath blessed us with all spiritual blessings in heavenly places in Christ" (Eph. 1:3).

We propose studying the Epistle to the Ephesians with a view to discovering the New Testament standard of commitment as presented to us by the Apostle Paul. These opening words of the epistle not only give us a summary of the truth of the Gospel, but reveal, out of the depths of Paul's experience, what the true Christian life is.

The benediction here corresponds to the apostolic benediction. We have first *the grace of our Lord Jesus Christ.* "The God and Father of our Lord Jesus Christ hath blessed us with all spiritual blessings *in Christ.*" The expression *in Christ* is the keynote of the epistle, occurring more than twenty times. The words of our text are the beginning of a sentence running nonstop from verses 3 to 14, in which we find "chosen in him," "foreordained through him," "accepted in him," "redemption in him," "the purpose of God in him," "summing up all things in him," "made an heritage in him," "in whom we believed," "in whom we were

25

sealed with the Holy Spirit." All our blessings are stored up
in Christ; and we ourselves are in Him, too.

As truly as the blessings are in Christ, so truly is our life
in Him. Life and blessing are inseparably intertwined.
Abiding in Christ means abiding in the heavenly places and
in all the spiritual blessings with which God has blessed us
in Him. Faith in Christ is meant to be nothing less than unceasing dependence and fellowship with Him and receiving
from Him every grace the soul can possibly need. As absolute and continuous as is the contact with the air which my
physical life needs, so *can my soul be kept in fellowship
with my Lord Jesus.* This is what Scripture means by the
words: "Christ is our life," "Christ liveth in me," "To me to
live is Christ." What riches of grace!

Next comes *the love of God.* It is the Father who has
blessed us in the Son. Christ was the Father's gift to us, and
all blessings are given by Him in the same intensity and
reality of possession. God's purpose was to bring us back to
himself as our Creator, in whose fellowship and glory our
happiness could alone be found. God could attain His object and satisfy the love of His own heart only by bringing
us into complete union with Christ himself, so that in Him
we can be as near to God as Christ is. Oh, the mystery of the
love of God!

Of all the blessings that we have in Christ, our text says,
"God hath blessed us with all spiritual blessings." More
than one believer, as he longed and prayed earnestly for
some new revelation of God's grace, has found in these
words the very key that he needs to unlock the treasury of
blessing. As the light of the Spirit shone upon these words,
they came alive with meaning. In Christ *God blessed me*
with all spiritual blessings. I only need the rest of faith to
accept and the wholehearted surrender to claim them in
Him. Then, the heart finds itself in the very center of blessing.

Such a sight of what is meant, and such a faith in

claiming it, can only lead to the adoring benediction: "Blessed be the God and Father of our Lord Jesus Christ." As it is the fountain from which the stream of blessings flows, so it may be in our life, too, an unceasing song of praise: "I will bless the Lord at all times; his praise shall continually be in my mouth" (Ps. 34:1).

We have thirdly, *the fellowship of the Spirit.* The spiritual blessings are nothing less than Holy-Spirit-blessings. As God, proceeding from the Father and the Son, He has the divine office of conveying and imparting to us all the fullness of blessing and blessedness in the divine life. He reveals them to us. He enables us to see and delight in and accept them. He communicates them so truly in our inmost being that we become spiritual men, clothed and filled with the power of the Spirit.

When the heart is fully surrendered to Him, He not only exercises a certain influence in us, but dwells within us in a divine reality and power that makes our heart the dwelling place of Christ and of God. He imparts to us, as a seed within us, every grace and virtue that there is in Christ, to become our own. What He reveals He also works. Just as the seed sown in the earth needs the warmth of the sun and the rain from heaven to make it grow, even so, as we believe that the seeds are within us, we look up to Christ in whom our life is; and in the sunshine of His love, the spiritual blessings grow up and are worked into our very being. In every blessing we have the whole of the blessed Trinity: the Father, the Son and the Holy Spirit.

In the epistle the Holy Spirit is mentioned twelve times in different aspects of the wonderful work He does in the believer. As we proceed to study these, the humble seeker will find a wonderful revelation of what God really meant the life of His children to be and how wonderfully He has provided that we should indeed attain to it. If we truly desire to discover the New Testament standard of true spiritual religion and the commitment in our life which God has made possible for us, we shall find in the Holy Spirit the courage needed for setting aside every human standard and making God's purpose our only aim.

Let us begin by taking the opening benediction which reveals to us the true life of spiritual blessing. We need to make this our own. Let us in quiet meditation wait upon the Holy Spirit to work in our inmost consciousness the faith that is in accordance with one whom the Father has blessed in Christ with every spiritual blessing. I humbly take my place before Him and say, "Blessed be God, Blessed be God!"

Many complain about the lack of spiritual life, and many prayers for its deepening are being made. Yet, there is profound ignorance as to what is really needed to bring a feeble Christian to a strong and joyous life in Christ Jesus. Let us learn from our text that nothing can better meet our need than the adoring worship of the ever-blessed Trinity. It is upon God, who has blessed us in Christ Jesus, on whom our expectation is to rest. It is in Christ that God and His blessings are to be found if we continue in close and unceasing fellowship with Him. It is through the Holy Spirit that the presence of the Father and the Son in divine power can be known.

The Holy Spirit has been given to make Christ real to us and to take every spiritual blessing and make it ours. A life entirely committed to the Holy Spirit, a heart full of faith and confidence that God and Christ and the Holy Spirit will do their wondrous work within us, a body yielded to God as a holy, living sacrifice on the altar for His service, will surely be accepted. God will teach us to sing the song of praise, "Blessed be the God and Father of our Lord Jesus Christ, who hath blessed us with all spiritual blessings in heavenly places in Christ!"

CHAPTER FIVE

The Sealing of the Spirit

"In whom also after that ye believed, ye were sealed with that Holy Spirit of promise" (Eph. 1:13).

The wonderful sentence that began with the spiritual blessing with which God has blessed us in Christ and which through ten verses showed us what we have in Him closes with that in which all is contained, the blessed sealing of the Holy Spirit. When a king appoints an ambassador or a governor, his commission is sealed with the king's seal, bearing the king's likeness. The Holy Spirit is the seal of our redemption, not in the sense of giving us the assurance of our sonship as something apart from himself: *He himself* by His life in us is the seal of our sonship. His work is to reveal and glorify Christ in us, the image of the Father, and by fixing our heart and our faith on Him, to transform us into His likeness. What a wonderful thought! The Spirit of the Father and the Son, the bond of our union with them, giving us the witness of the divine life within us, and enabling us to live out that life daily. In the Christian life everything depends on knowing the presence of the Holy Spirit and understanding His blessed work.

First, we need to know that He comes to take the mastery of our whole person—spirit, soul, and body—and

29

through it to reveal the life and the power of God as it works in our renewed personality. Just as Christ could not be glorified and receive the Spirit from the Father for us until He had died upon the cross—parting with that life in which He had borne our sin and weaknesses—so, the coming of the Holy Spirit into our hearts in power implies that we yield ourselves to the fellowship of the Cross, and consent to die entirely to that life in which self and sin have their power. Through the death of the self-life comes the Holy Spirit, the heavenly life to take complete possession of us.

This entire mastery implies on our side complete surrender and obedience. Peter speaks of the "Holy Ghost, whom God hath given to them that obey him." Even as Christ came to do God's will alone and humbled himself to the perfect obedience of the cross that He might receive the Spirit from the Father and we through Him, so the full experience of the Spirit's power rests entirely on our readiness in everything to deny self, in everything to yield ourselves to His teaching and leading. The reason that believers are feeble and ignorant of the blessings of the Spirit is this: At conversion and in their Christian life the question was never faced and settled that by the grace of God they would in everything, in every place, and at every moment yield themselves to the control of the Spirit. Oh, that God's children would accept God's terms: *the undivided mastery of the Spirit, the unhesitating surrender of the whole being to His control.*

In this connection, we need to understand that the degree or measure in which the working of the Spirit is experienced may vary greatly. A believer may rejoice in one of the fruit of the Spirit (peace or joy, zeal or boldness) and yet be extremely deficient in the other graces which His presence bestows. Our position toward the blessed Spirit must be that of perfect teachableness, waiting to be led by Him in all the will of God. There must be the consciousness of how much there still is within the heart that needs to be renewed and sanctified if He is to have the place and the honor that belong to Him.

There are two great enemies under which man was brought by his fall: the world and self. Of the world Christ says, "The Spirit of truth, whom the world cannot receive because it knoweth him not." *Worldliness is the great hindrance that keeps believers from living the spiritual life.* Of self Christ said, "Let a man deny himself," "Let a man hate his own life." *Self, in all its forms—self-will, self-pleasing, self-confidence—renders a life in the power of the Spirit impossible.* From these two great enemies, the power of the world and the power of self, nothing can deliver us but the Cross of Christ. Paul boasts in the Cross by which he has been crucified to the world. He tells us, "They that are Christ's have crucified the flesh," in which self has its seat of power. Living in the spiritual life must begin with the entire surrender of the old life to death, to make room for the blessed Spirit to renew and transform our whole being into the will of God.

Apart from the Holy Spirit, nothing we do is acceptable to God. "No man can say that Jesus is Lord but by the Holy Ghost." No man can truly say, "Abba, Father," but by the Spirit of God's Son sent into his heart. In our fellowship with God, in our fellowship with men, in our worship and our daily work, in the highest pursuit that life can offer and in the daily care of our bodies, *everything must bear the seal of the Holy Spirit.*

Of the Son we read, "Him hath God the Father sealed." It is "in Christ" that we are sealed. Just as Jesus Christ was led by the Holy Spirit throughout His entire life—a life that led to the cross, "where by the eternal Spirit he offered himself a sacrifice unto God"—so we are to live our daily life as those who are sealed by the Spirit. As true as it is of Christ, so it is true of every believer—the Son, and every son, sealed by the Father. The New Testament standard of the Christian life and its commitment is that the whole life is to bear the stamp of the Holy Spirit.

Let us learn the precious lesson that the Holy Spirit cannot inspire our devotional life unless He inspires our daily life. The Spirit of Christ claims and needs the rule of the whole man if He is to perform His blessed work in us. The indwelling of the Holy Spirit means that in the entirety of our life, nothing is to be thought of, or trusted to, or sought after, but the immediate and continual dependence on His blessed working. The commitment expressed by our public life will be the test of the uprightness of our private devotion and at the same time the means of strengthening our confidence in the God who works in us through His blessed Spirit. Every thought of faith in the power of the Spirit must find its expression in prayer to God, who will most surely give us His Spirit when we ask Him and work in us through the Spirit what we need.

A seal, attached to a document, gives validity to every sentence and every word it contains. Even so, the Holy Spirit of promise, with which we are sealed, confirms every promise that there is in Christ. This pictures one of the great differences between the Bible and the human standard of the Christian life. The Bible standard pictures the seal of the Spirit being accepted in His control of every movement and every moment of our life. The human standard pictures us as content with a very partial surrender to His guidance.

CHAPTER SIX

The Spirit of Wisdom

"I cease not to give thanks for you, making mention of
you in my prayers; that . . . the Father of glory may give
unto you the spirit of wisdom and revelation in the knowledge of him: the eyes of your understanding being enlight-
ened; that ye may know. . ." (Eph. 1:16-18).

No sooner had Paul mentioned the Holy Spirit, as God's
seal on believers, than he speaks of his unceasing prayer
that God would give them a spirit of wisdom. It is not
enough that the believer has the Holy Spirit; that Spirit can
only do His blessed work as God works through Him in answer to prayer. Paul prays unceasingly, and with that
teaches believers to pray unceasingly for the wisdom of the
Holy Spirit to enlighten the eyes of their heart. Just as a
child needs education, the believer who has the indwelling
Spirit needs divine illumination from day to day to know
God and the spiritual life He bestows. This life is so supernatural and such a divine mystery that without spiritual
wisdom and understanding we cannot apprehend it.[1]

We need to know three things. First, what "the hope of
his calling" is; the high and holy and heavenly calling of
which we are to walk worthily. Then, "the riches of the

33

glory of God's inheritance in the saints"; what the unsearchable riches are of the heavenly treasure which God
has in His saints. And last, "the power" by which we can
fulfill our calling and possess our inheritance: "the exceeding greatness of his power to us-ward who believe."

The life of the Christian is to be the life of God in the human soul—nothing we can do will maintain that life or renew it. It is a life that we have in Christ; it is a life to be received from Christ by faith daily and hourly; it is a life
which the omnipotence of God himself alone can begin and
carry on. The great need of the believer is to wait upon God
for the Holy Spirit to show "the exceeding greatness of his
power to us-ward who believe." No human mind can grasp
it; the Holy Spirit living in the heart reveals it, and teaches
us to believe it and expect it. As Christians we need to depend upon God daily to work in us according to His power
and every day to accept the Holy Spirit's teaching in answer to prayer.[2]

With regard to this mighty power dwelling in us, only
the Holy Spirit can show us what its work and nature is. It
is the power of God, "according to the working of his mighty
power, which he wrought in Christ, when he raised him
from the dead, and set him at his own right hand." It is this
power that works in us who believe and raises us up from a
life under the power of death to a life in the glory of heaven.
It is by the exceeding greatness of this power that our daily
life is to be lived, in fellowship with the life of the Son of
God.

God raised Christ from the dead because His death on
the cross had been that of the most perfect obedience. Because He had yielded himself unreservedly to the power of
God, both in His life and suffering, and in His surrender to
death and the grave, God raised Him from the dead and
gave Him glory. Even so, when we give ourselves over to die
with Christ to sin and the world and the flesh, in a Christlike humility and obedience, the exceeding greatness of His

power will work in us to make us partakers, day by day, of the resurrection power and of the Spirit of glory which follows it.

This thought of the life of the believer as being the exhibition of "the exceeding greatness of his power to us-ward who believe" runs through all the writings of Paul. In his prayer for the Colossians (1:10), he asks that they may "walk worthy of the Lord unto all pleasing, being fruitful in every good work, and increasing in the knowledge of God." Then he adds, "strengthened with all might, according to his glorious power, unto all patience and longsuffering with joyfulness."

As one thinks of the life of commitment which Paul upholds, always worthy of God and pleasing to him, always fruitful in every good work, always increasing in the knowledge of God, and always persevering with all patience and long-suffering, it appears from the natural standpoint that the standard is an impossible one. But then the thought comes, "strengthened with all might, according to his glorious power." We say in answer to the natural, "No, if this be true, if God works this, the life is possible."

In Ephesians the same thought occurs (3:20): "Now unto him that is able to do exceeding abundantly above all that we ask or think, according to the power that worketh in us, unto him be glory in the church by Christ Jesus throughout all ages." The words lift our hearts to believe and expect something far beyond what we ask or think. The life we are to live is to be a supernatural one; it is to be the resurrection life; *the heavenly life of Christ in glory maintained in us by the same working of the strength of His might* by which He raised Christ from the cross to the throne. The very same almighty power by which Christ was raised from the dead as the conqueror of sin and death is the power that works in our hearts to give us the victory over every sin. To believe this with our whole heart will at once bring us to a sense of our utter inability, but also of the divine certainty that God will fulfill His purpose in us.

If the believer will but trust the exceeding greatness of His power; will but yield himself in entire submission to allow that power to rule in his heart and to do all its will there; if he will be content to trust the strength that is made perfect in weakness; if he will but count all things as loss for the sake of this blessed prize—God's Word has promised that the power that raised Christ will work in him day by day until he knows how to presently live and reign with Christ in glory.

We are trying to discover what the New Testament standard of a life of true commitment is and whether the accepted standard of modern Christianity is in harmony with it. Let us summarize in our own minds the full meaning of Paul's prayer. Think of his private devotional pleading for his Ephesians. Think of the standard of his own life, as he speaks so often of God's working in him (Col. 1:29; 1 Cor. 5:10; 2 Cor. 3:5; 4:7; 12:9, 10; Phil. 4:13). Think of what he wished his readers to take as their goal and expectation in life.

Paul's entire soul was focused upon the two great thoughts: every believer living every day under the teaching of the Holy Spirit and under the mighty power of God working in him. Pause and ask whether your private devotion, your confident faith, and your hope in daily life have been centered in and rejoice in the life that is held out to us here—daily to live out the exceeding greatness of God's power working in you, and daily to yield yourself to the Holy Spirit in dependence upon His power.[3]

May God help us to return again and again to this passage until it becomes to us the very light of God shining in our heart and the power of God working in our life!

CHAPTER SEVEN
The Spirit of Access

"Through him we both have access by one Spirit unto the Father" (Eph. 2:18; cf. 3:12).

Have you ever noticed the beauty of the passage that leads up to the words of our text? In verses 4-10, we have the declaration of the great salvation which God has granted to us. This is contained in the words, "By grace are ye saved through faith." From this section we gather six qualities concerning Christian living and commitment.

1. *It is a present reality:* "Ye are saved—God hath quickened us together with Christ—And raised us up together—And made us to sit together in the heavenly places—We are his workmanship, created in Christ Jesus unto good works." What a salvation, all the work of God in us!

2. *It is "by grace":* That points to what had been said—"God, who is rich in mercy—For his great love wherewith he loved us—That in the ages to come [that is, from the resurrection onward], he might show the exceeding riches of his grace—In his kindness toward us through Christ Jesus." What richness and glory in God's grace!

3. *It is "through faith":* "Not of yourselves—It is the

gift of God—Not of works—Created in Christ Jesus unto good works, which God before ordained." What a salvation and what a grace prepared for faith to receive and live in!

Then follows (vv. 11-17) the way in which these Gentiles had been led to the knowledge of that salvation. "Made nigh by the blood of Christ," with Christ their peace destroying the enmity and reconciling Jew and Gentile in one body unto God through the cross. And so we reach our text: "For through him we both have access by one Spirit unto the Father." Here again, we have the blessed Trinity with the precious lesson that the great work in which Christ and the Holy Spirit are united is to make the permanent and unceasing presence of God a blessed reality. Our text not only speaks of a right of access, but of its actual enjoyment as secured to us through Christ and His Spirit.

4. *It brings us into "access to the Father"*: Think of what Scripture teaches us. In the tabernacle, the Holiest of all was separated by a thick veil from the Holy Place, in which the priest came daily to serve. Not even the High Priest was allowed to enter that Holiest of all, except on one day of the year. The Holiest of all was the dwelling place of God. Access through the veil was forbidden and punishable by death. When Christ died, this veil was rent. Christ Jesus not only entered into God's presence with His blood, but He opened a new and living way through the rent veil of His flesh for us to enter. When the veil was rent in the tabernacle, the way was opened to all the priests. When Jesus entered heaven, the way was opened for every believer to enter into God's holy presence, not for a time, but to dwell there every day and all the day. Jesus sent the Holy Spirit from heaven to bring us into that holy presence and to enable us to live in it. The unbroken enjoyment of God's presence is possible to every believer who will forsake all to possess it.

5. *It is "through the Son"*: That does not only mean as our Advocate, who secures our pardon and acceptance. It means much more. Our High Priest lives and acts in the

power of an endless, incorruptible life. He works in us by the power of His resurrection life, the life of heaven itself. To have access to God through Christ means that as those "quickened together with Christ . . . and made [to] sit together in the heavenly places," we live in Him, we are one with Him, we abide in Him, and are by Him ever brought and kept in the fellowship with God. *The access through Christ brings us as near to God as Christ is, in an intimate, divine fellowship that passes all understanding.*

6. *It is "in one Spirit"*: The Spirit has been given to us that we may have the power to cry, "Abba, Father," even as Christ did. The Spirit dwells in us to reveal Christ; without Him, no man can truthfully call Jesus Lord. The Spirit takes control of our whole life and being; where He is yielded to and trusted, He maintains the fellowship with the Father through the Son, in the Holiest of all, a divine reality in our life.

This is the New Testament standard of Christian living: entrance and access to God's holy presence and love through the living union with Christ in the power of the Holy Spirit. The one thing needed to make it ours is the practice of the presence of God—the continual yielding of our life to the prompting of the Holy Spirit. It must be a life of access through Christ in the Spirit, restoring to us what Adam had lost in the fall, a walk in the light of God. This walk must be as clear and natural as is the enjoyment of the sun to our bodies. No thinking, no feeling and no working can enable us to dispense with the actual exercise, day by day, of the privilege of access into the Holiest of all and of dwelling there.

Most of us are familiar with the hymn, "Take Time To Be Holy." I was struck by the use of this expression in the *Life of Griffith John.* After being in China more than twenty years, he often said to young missionaries, "Preach the Gospel, and take time to be holy as the preparation." In the Mission Conference in Shanghai in 1877, he said, "The missionary must above everything be a holy man; the Chinese expect it of him. I am persuaded that no minister can be a great spiritual power in whom this is not in good measure seen. He must be more than a good man; a man who takes time, not only to master the language and the literature of the people, but to be holy. . . . Brethren, this is what we need if this empire is to be moved by us. To this end the throne of grace must be our refuge; the shadow of the Almighty must every day and every hour be our dwelling, we must take time to be filled with His power, we must take time to be holy."

It is only he who will avail himself fully to the access to the Holiest of all, where God dwells and reveals himself through Christ in the Spirit, on whom the blessed truth will dawn that full fellowship with God in His holiness will make us holy too. It is in this inner chamber of God's presence that the school of true commitment will be taught.

Take time with God, the triune Holy One. Take time with the Father, of whom it is said: "The God of peace himself sanctify you wholly. Faithful is he which calleth you, who also will do it." Take time with Christ, the Holy One of God, who said, "Holy Father, for their sakes I sanctify myself, that they themselves also may be sanctified in truth." Take time with the Holy Spirit, the Spirit of God's holiness, making you His holy temple. Give time to this holy fellowship; God himself will sanctify you wholly. Live in the unbroken experience. Through Christ we have our access in one Spirit unto the Father.

CHAPTER EIGHT

The Temple of the Spirit

"Jesus Christ himself being the chief corner stone; in whom all the building fitly framed together groweth unto an holy temple in the Lord: in whom ye also are builded together for an habitation of God through the Spirit" (Eph. 2:20-22).

We have again in the text the blessed Trinity. The Father, God, for whom the dwelling place is built. The Son, Jesus Christ, the chief cornerstone, in whom the holy temple grows. The Spirit, the builder, through whom all the living stones are united with each other and with the chief cornerstone, and thus in perfect fellowship with God. As in heaven, so in the Church on earth and in the heart of every believer, the triune Holy One is the God of our salvation.

The great thought of the passage is fellowship—the fellowship of the Spirit as seen in the temple. That fellowship is spoken of first as the fellowship of believers, built up into one holy temple. Paul had spoken of the Gentiles as strangers from the covenant of the promise, who are now brought near in the blood of Christ; of the enmity being abolished and nailed to the cross, that we both might have access in one Spirit to the Father. In verse 19 he says, "Ye are no more strangers and foreigners, but fellow-citizens with the saints, and of the household of God." As Jew and Gentile both had access by one Spirit to the Father, so by the same Spirit they are built into one temple. The cross has ended all separation among men: Jews and Gentiles, Greek and barbarian, the wise and the foolish—all are one in Christ Jesus. National and social distinctions are as nothing compared to that unity which the Spirit gives in Christ Jesus. The cement by which the living stones are held together, the bond by which all are the members of one household and one body is nothing less than the Spirit and the life and the love of God himself.

Fellowship with Christ, the cornerstone, is also the work of the blessed Spirit. In Him the believer on earth and the Father in heaven find their bond of union. We will surely suffer if we regard as an end what is only a means. Men think of pardon and peace, obedience and holiness as an end, while they are only the means to the great goal of bringing God and man into perfect union. When we speak of the Mosaic worship, we prize and press the thought of the atonement through blood and the access of the High Priest to sprinkle the blood on the mercy seat. We see in these the shadow of what Christ has done for us; yet, we forget there was something higher—nothing less than the presence and fellowship of God himself. God dwelt in the sanctuary in the midst of His people that He might be their God and that they might enjoy His guidance, His blessing, His mighty deliverance in their time of need, and His abiding presence. This is what we need to fix our hearts on God's Word: that *fellowship with the Father and the Son, that communion, intimate, holy, and unceasing, is what man was created for and has been restored to in Christ Jesus.*

As believers accept and realize their dependence on Christ, their inseparable union with Him, and trust the blessed Spirit ever to maintain within them His presence, they will come to know that the presence and the power of

God is the highest of all the blessings with which He has blessed us in Christ Jesus.

In the apostolic benediction, "the fellowship of the Holy Spirit" indicates what His chief work is. Through Him alone we have our access in Christ to the Father. He reveals Christ to us, the reality of our union with Him, and the nearness to God which He gives. He not only builds the temple but reveals the indwelling God. He not only builds the temple as a whole but makes each heart a temple and reveals how God is willing and able to be and to do in our hearts what He is and does in His heaven above. What so many Christians think is an impossibility, that the presence of God himself can be with them and can keep them all the day, is indeed possible if we know and believe in the Holy Spirit as the power of God that works in us.

Fellowship with God, with Christ the chief cornerstone, and with each other constitutes the blessedness of our being built as a dwelling place of God in the Spirit. We need to know that in the Cross of Christ all selfishness has been destroyed and that the love that seeks no life but giving itself for others has been made possible to us. This understanding will reveal that a close fellowship with each other is as sacred and indispensable as fellowship with God. We will not only see how utterly our spiritual life depends upon it, but how there is no way of proving to men our love to God and the reality of God's love to us except through the love of the brethren. When our Lord Jesus prayed "that they may be one, even as we are one . . . that the world may know that thou hast loved them . . . as thou hast loved me," He taught us that a divided church is powerless before the enemy. Only a love for the brethren like God's and Christ's will give us the victory. When they see it, the world will be compelled to acknowledge that Christ crucified is verily present and working in us. It has been said, "If without recognizing the unity of the Body, pentecostal power were again to be made manifest, the churches would appropriate the glory to themselves, and would not lay it down at the feet of the King."

The New Testament standard of the spiritual life must be lifted up and love for the brethren must take the place that God's Word has given it. This is the only proof of the reality of our love to God and of the conformity of our life to the image of Jesus Christ and His love on the cross. Then, our private devotions will be delivered from the selfishness that so often hinders them. Our hearts will sense a new confidence that God will hear the prayers which the Spirit teaches us to plead for the growing of a holy temple in the Lord, a worthy dwelling place of God in the Spirit. And we shall learn that the power of the Holy Spirit and our commitment to Him can be the distinctive mark of our life all the day.

CHAPTER NINE

The Spirit of Missions

"The mystery of Christ . . . as it is now revealed unto his holy apostles and prophets by the Spirit; that the Gentiles should be fellow-heirs, and of the same body, and partakers of his promise in Christ by the gospel" (Eph. 3:4-6).

Studying the Epistle to the Ephesians, one becomes deeply impressed that the New Testament standard of Christian commitment is but faintly realized in the Church. Its whole tone is intensely supernatural. Christian commitment or devotedness involves a life totally identified with the life of Christ. To fulfill its meaning, it must be a life under the unceasing presence and guidance of the Holy Spirit.

In the first chapter of our epistle, Paul set before us the source of the divine life, followed by the unceasing prayer that that life might be revealed by the Holy Spirit in the hearts of his readers. In chapter two we had the communication of that life, God himself making us alive in Christ and making us His workmanship, created in Christ Jesus for good works. Now, in chapter three we are taught that the proclamation of that divine life is equally the work of God and His Spirit. As definitely as the origin and communication of His life is a supernatural one, so the provision for its being proclaimed in the world is entirely supernatural.

We have here the exceeding glory of God's grace set before us in a new light. In chapter one we had "his grace, wherein he hath made us accepted in the beloved . . . the forgiveness of sins, according to the riches of his grace." In chapter two we had "the exceeding riches of his grace in his kindness toward us through Jesus Christ." Now, in chapter three we have "the dispensation of the grace of God which . . . is now revealed unto his holy apostles and prophets by the Spirit," and of which Paul was made a minister "according to the gift of the grace of God unto me by the effectual working of his power." In the ministry of the gospel, the riches of God's grace are to be notably manifested and magnified. Paul speaks of the "mystery of Christ" that has now been revealed by the Holy Spirit—that the Gentiles are fellow heirs, and fellow members, and fellow partakers in Christ Jesus. Of this mystery he has been made a minister.

As it was through the Spirit that the revelation of what had been hid in God through the ages was revealed, so it was under the presence and direction of the Holy Spirit that the work of bringing the Gospel to every creature was begun and to be carried out. We read in Acts, "the Spirit said" to Philip to speak to the man of Ethiopia; "the Spirit said to Peter" to go to Cornelius; "the Holy Ghost said" to the praying company at Antioch, "Separate me Barnabas and Saul." "It seemed good to the Holy Ghost" that liberty should be given to the Gentiles in Antioch. We read of Paul "being forbidden of the Holy Ghost" to speak the Word in Asia, and of "the Spirit of Jesus not suffering" them to go into Bithynia. Paul speaks of what Christ worked through him for the obedience of the Gentiles "in the power of the Holy Ghost," and that his ministering the Gospel to the Gentiles might be acceptable, "being sanctified by the Holy Ghost." Elsewhere, he speaks of his preaching among the

Gentiles as being "in power and in the Holy Ghost and in much assurance," even as they also "received the word with joy of the Holy Ghost."

To the Holy Spirit was entrusted the entire ministry of revealing and carrying out through the succeeding ages the riches of the glory of this mystery among the Gentiles— "Christ in you, the hope of glory." All mission work has been placed under the direction of the Holy Spirit; in every department of that work His guidance is to be sought for and counted upon. Missions are indeed the work of the Holy Spirit (Acts 1:8).

We may well ask why so little use is made of these references to the Holy Spirit regarding missions. It is to be feared that it may be due to a lack of living faith in the Holy Spirit. It is the work of the Holy Spirit to reveal the great mystery of God in the heart, to awaken its affections and its purpose, and to empower for all the service that is needed to carry out God's blessed will. It is not enough that to the prophets and the apostles, to preachers and believers of true commitment, the Spirit should reveal this hidden mystery of God. The result would be that the Church as a whole would only become acquainted with His plans. Everyone who hears needs individually to receive the teaching of the Spirit if the blessed secret is really to master and possess them.

We count it a great advancement when a church or a congregation has yielded itself to the call to take a part in the great work of evangelizing the nations. Unfortunately, this may stem from nothing more than a sense of duty and a readiness to take a part in all the activities of the church. Much more is needed if believers are to be brought under the great truth that missions is the chief purpose of the Church. It is the only goal for which every congregation and, therefore, every individual believer exists. When the Holy Spirit is honored and waited upon, when in preaching and in writing, in prayer and in Christian dialogue, when

all the work within the church is to train for her great calling to win the lost for Christ, there is still one prerequisite:
the dependence upon the Holy Spirit must be counted as
the first and essential element of success. Only then will the
Church be able to carry out its Lord's commands. When the
Holy Spirit, in our missionary committees and meetings
and conferences, takes the place that was given to Him in
the Apostolic Church, we may expect that His power will be
manifested as in the early days.

"Ye shall receive power, after that the Holy Ghost is
come upon you; and ye shall be witnesses unto me . . . to
the uttermost part of the earth." These were the very last
words of our Lord before His ascension. They linked the
promise of the Spirit with the ends of the earth. *The fullness of the Spirit will be given only in connection with the
extension of the Kingdom.* The power for carrying the Gospel to those both near or far is absolutely dependent upon
the measure of the Spirit's presence. Every prayer for the
power of the Spirit should have as its goal the power to tes-
tify for Jesus. As the number of believers who have power to
prevail with God in prayer for the Spirit's increase, so will
the Church be strengthened for preaching the Gospel to
every creature.

The connection between these thoughts and our life of
private devotion is close and vital. Paul spoke to believers
of "the conflict" he had in unceasing prayer for the
churches among the lost, even for those he had not yet seen.
He asked them "to labour and strive with him in prayer"
for his work of preaching to the Gentiles. Prayer was not
only to be for the supply of the needs of the spiritual life,
but also a training school for the exercise of the highest
powers of our being in God's service. Prayer is conflict with
the powers of darkness, a fellowship with the Cross and its
intercession, a stirring up of our strength to take hold of
God and to prevail with Him for His blessing on men
around us. When the prayer consciousness grows, "I have

power with God; He will listen to me; He will give an answer," then our mission work will become more than ever a triumph of the Cross in its power in our own life, before the throne of heaven, and on the battlefield for the lost.

Let us test our devotional life by the influence it really exercises on the fulfillment of the msytery of Christ in the world. Let us believe that in the inner chamber the work can be done that will count for eternity, and that there the power can be received that will make itself felt in whatever sphere God positions us in for the establishment of His Kingdom upon earth. Let us not fear to say what Paul said of himself, "Unto me, who am less than the least of all saints, is this grace given, to make known unto the Gentiles the unsearchable riches of Christ."

May our commitment always be a wholehearted yielding to the blessed Spirit. We may rely upon Him to lead us into the riches of the glory of this mystery among the Gentiles. And our prayer will increasingly be for the power of the Holy Spirit to permeate all that is being done for mission work, whether within the Church or through it among the lost.

CHAPTER TEN

The Spirit of Power

"I bow my knees unto the Father . . . that he would grant you, according to the riches of his glory, to be strengthened with might by his Spirit in the inner man, that Christ may dwell in your hearts by faith" (Eph. 3:14-17).

Once again, we have in this wonderful prayer the blessed Trinity: the Father granting the Spirit of power; the Spirit revealing Christ in the heart; that through Christ and the Spirit we may be filled unto all the fullness of God! As God dwells in heaven as the triune One, even so in our hearts.[1]

In the prayer at the close of chapter one, we had the Spirit of wisdom that we might know God in the exceeding greatness of His power to us who believe. In chapter three we have the prayer for the Spirit of power to strengthen us with might; the exceeding greatness of God's power is to be the unceasing experience in our inner life. Let us bow with deep reverence as we gaze upon this mystery of love.

Notice the expression, "that he would grant you according to the riches of his glory." Paul wants us to take time and think of God's glory and of His inconceivable riches. In faith Paul would have us expect that God will do nothing less for us than the standard of the riches of that glory. What is to be done in our inner man is to be of the same essence as the glory of God. He means to shine that glory into our hearts and manifest the riches of His power in what He does there within us. Our faith should not expect the fulfillment of this prayer until it enters into and claims that God will do in us "according to the riches of his glory." Let us take time and see that nothing less than this is the standard of our faith.

This is to be our expectation: "that he would grant you . . . to be strengthened with might by his Spirit in the inner man." The Holy Spirit is indeed the mighty power of God. As the Spirit of wisdom, He reveals the exceeding greatness of God's power that lifted Christ from the cross to the throne. First, He must teach us to see and desire and believe in this exceeding greatness of God's power in us; then, as the Spirit of power, He works in us, strengthening us with power in the inner man.

In His Word, God continually calls upon His servants to be strong and of good courage. God chooses the weak things of this world; but when once they are truly weak, He wants them to be strong in faith and strong in the power of His might. He wants to equip them with strength of will, ready to do all that God says, and with strength of character be bold for any sacrifice. Just as in a healthy body the strength is not something separated from the whole but fills the entire being, so to be strengthened with power by the Spirit in the inner man means that our whole nature and being is under the sway of His mighty, life-giving power.

The object of this strengthening with might is threefold. First of all, "that Christ may dwell in your hearts by faith." The divine power enables and equips our faith to claim this precious privilege of the fulfillment of the promise in John 14. In the prayer in chapter one the Holy Spirit by the power of God was to reveal Christ to us as the object of our faith. Here the Savior comes nearer; the Spirit reveals Him dwelling within us and gives the consciousness of His unceasing and all-powerful presence. Just as God maintains the life of the body by supporting the heart in its action, so the Holy Spirit, by His almighty power, strengthens our inward man day by day to enable us to live the spiritual life in reality. Christ's dwelling in the heart is meant to be our strength.[2]

Then comes the second promise. Related to the indwelling of Christ, we are "rooted and grounded in love," and comprehend something of the reality and the joy of the love of Christ that surpasses human knowledge.

This leads on to "being filled with the fulness of God"—the Spirit of power filling the inner man, the presence of Christ filling the heart, the fullness of God extending into the depths of our personalities.

No wonder that Paul says, "Now unto him that is able to do exceeding abundantly above all that we ask or think, according to the power that worketh in us, unto him be glory . . . throughout all ages." The faith in the promise of what the Father of glory will do, according to the riches of His glory, will teach us to worship in deep prostration, in which we can only say, "Glory, glory to Him for ever and ever."

This doxology is in reality a revelation of the root of Paul's standard of prayer and expectation and attainment. He was filled with one thought: what he had asked in the prayer concerning the strengthening by God's power and in agreement with the riches of God's glory was an experience that could and would be granted. He knew that many would say that the prayer was meant to be an ideal to stir our desires, but that its actual fulfillment in life in this world was beyond our reach. Such a thought would cut away the very root of faith in the supernatural power of God as being what is absolutely secured in the promise, and therefore possible in experience. Paul dares any reader to declare that what he had asked for out of the riches of God's glory—the strengthening with divine power, the continual indwelling of Christ in the heart, such a rooting in love as to know the love of Christ which exceeds human understanding, and as to be filled with all the fullness of God—is too high and beyond what we dare think or ask. He knew that in the same measure of what the exceeding greatness of God's power had done and was doing in his own life, God was ready to do in anyone who would give himself unreservedly in heart and life to God. He answers every doubt and encourages every sincere believer to trust God for the fulfillment of the prayer and to say with him: "Now unto him"—let us pause and say with him humbly and reverently—"Now unto him that is able to do exceeding abundantly above all that we ask or think, according to the power that worketh in us, unto him be glory . . . by Christ Jesus, world without end. Amen."

Here is Paul's standard of the New Testament life. Is it ours? Do I believe it with my whole heart and soul? Does it transform my private devotion in prayer? Does it inspire my life commitment as the grandest thing there is in the world?

Let us return to the opening words: "I bow my knees to the Father," and plead for ourselves. It is our responsibility as God's people to receive the strengthening with power according to the riches of His glory. God waits to do it. Who will wait to receive it?

What is more, who will yield himself, like Paul, to be an intercessor? Who will plead with and for the believers around him that they may learn to expect the almighty power of God to work in them? Who will plead that what has appeared beyond their reach may become the object of their longing desire and their confident assurance—a life of faith in which Christ in the heart shall live in them?

CHAPTER ELEVEN

The Unity of the Spirit

"I . . . beseech you that ye walk worthy of the vocation wherewith ye are called, with all lowliness and meekness, with longsuffering, forbearing one another in love; endeavouring to keep the unity of the Spirit in the bond of peace" (Eph. 4:1-3).

The Epistle to the Ephesians is divided into two equal halves. In chapters one to three we have the divine life in its heavenly origin revealed in the heart of man by the Holy Spirit. In chapters four to six we have the Christian life in the ordinary conduct of our daily walk. The two halves correspond to what we said of commitment as an act and as a habit. The first three chapters begin with an act of adoration: "Blessed be God, who hath blessed us," and tell of what all those blessings are. They end with the ascription of glory to Him who is able to do above all that we can ask or think. In every act of prayer and praise, the soul takes its place in the midst of all those riches and seeks to enter more fully into their possession. The last three chapters begin with: "Walk worthy of your vocation [high calling]," and teach us how to demonstrate our commitment as a habit of the soul in the common actions of daily life. As in the

55

epistle, so in our experience, commitment lifts us up into the heavenly places to return to this earth so infused with its blessings that, in all our attitudes and actions, we may prove that our whole life is devoted to God alone.

The opening words of the second half bring us to the very roots of the Christian life: "Walk worthy of the vocation . . . with all lowliness and meekness . . . endeavouring to keep the unity of the Spirit in the bond of peace." The great mark of the call of Christ upon a believer is humility. In the following verse we have "one body and Spirit," and the further unveiling of what the Spirit does as the Spirit of unity. But in our text we have the unity of the Spirit as it is to be maintained in daily relationships with our fellow believers. In the midst of all diversity of character and all the temptations arising from the imperfections and evil of those around us, the first mark of true commitment, a life wholly devoted and given up to God, is this: "Walk . . . with all lowliness and meekness."

To realize the importance of this statement, first look at it in its connection with the first three chapters. Think of the heavenly blessings which God has blessed us with in Christ. Think of the exceeding greatness of His power to those who believe. Think of the Holy Spirit, by whom that power is to be revealed in us; through whom we have access to God in Christ, and are built up as a dwelling place of God; through whom we are to be mightily strengthened according to the riches of God's glory, so that Christ can dwell in our hearts. Think of the doxology concerning His ability to do exceeding abundantly above all that we can ask or think, according to the power that works in us—to make all these promises true in us. Take time, and form some true conception of the wonderful standard of spiritual life indicated in these words.

And, then, note the transition: "Walk worthy of this high calling in all lowliness and meekness." The fruit of this astonishing revelation of the grace of God, the one mark that you are truly a partaker of it, will be a deep and never ceasing humility. Humility will be the proof that God has come to you and revealed himself and brought everything like self and its pride down into the very dust.

If you would enter more deeply into the meaning of the words, just think that this lowliness and meekness do not comprise your disposition and attitude toward God only, but especially toward others. "In all lowliness and meekness, with longsuffering, forbearing one another in love." There is no clearer proof that God's spiritual blessings in Christ Jesus have reached and mastered a man than lowliness and meekness in his relationships with his fellowmen. The exceeding greatness of God's power in us who believe, raising us out of death to self and sin to Christ Jesus on the throne, "seated with him in the heavenly places," makes us like Christ, willing to wear servant's garments and to do servant's work. *What is impossible with men is possible with God.*

This same Christlike disposition is seen in Paul's words to the Philippians: "Let nothing be done through . . . vainglory; but in lowliness of mind let each esteem other better than themselves." The Master himself, the meek and lowly Lamb of God, had spoken, "Learn of me, for I am meek and lowly of heart." Paul enforces what he has written by adding, "Let this mind be in you, which was also in Christ Jesus." The Master emptied himself, taking the form of a servant, becoming obedient even unto death, even the death of the cross. The self-emptying of the heavenly glory, the form of a servant during all His earthly life, and then the humbling of himself to the death of the cross—such was the mind of Christ. Our salvation is rooted in this; it is in participation in this that salvation consists; it is in the spirit and practice of a life like this that Christ will be magnified and our hearts sanctified, and the true witness given that we have been with Jesus.

It is from this attitude that we derive our strength to

diligently keep the "unity of the Spirit in the bond of peace." It is not what we know, or think, or speak concerning the beauty of love and the unity of the Body and the power of the Holy Spirit that proves the true Christian life. It is in the meekness and lowliness of Christ, in daily relationship with our fellow Christians, even when they are a trial or disappointment to us, that we are to show our willingness to sacrifice anything to maintain the unity of the Spirit and to maintain the bond of love. Jesus' standard of service is a willingness to be the servant of all. It may not be easy; but Christ came from heaven to bring humility back to this earth and to work it out in our hearts.

Do we find in the teaching and preaching of the Church this lowliness and meekness of Christ as holding the place it does in the Word of God? In the fellowship of Christians, is there an endeavor to maintain this standard of Christian living and to keep the unity of the Spirit from being disturbed by pride or self? In our own life and our search after the deepening of the spiritual life, is this meekness and lowliness—so pleasing to God, so glorious as seen in Christ Jesus, so beautiful as a grace in a believer—our heart's desire and our confident hope? Oh, may it be in every act of commitment the first thing we ask of God, a heart humbled and brought low by His infinite love, and yielded to His Holy Spirit to work out in us and in His Body around us, the blessed likeness of Jesus our Lord. By the Spirit's help it can become the undercurrent and the habit of a life committed to God.

We are studying the work of the Holy Spirit. Let us not forget to link the thought of a Christlike lowliness with Him and His power. It was in the power of the Spirit that Christ was led to humble himself upon the cross as a sacrifice to God. It is only as we claim and receive and fully yield ourselves to the life of the Spirit that the meekness and lowliness of our Lord can be found in us. Let us believe mightily that He can and will indeed work it in us.

CHAPTER TWELVE
The Spirit of Unity

"There is one body and one Spirit" (Eph. 4:4).

In our last chapter our subject was the unity of the Spirit as it is to be maintained in our relationships with fellow Christians in all lowliness and meekness, with long-suffering, forbearing one another in love. Here our subject is the Spirit of unity, as He is the source and the power in which believers, as members of one body in Christ Jesus, are to minister to each other for the building up of the Body of Christ.

The knowledge of what the Body of Christ means, the insight into its glory and its purpose, and the fulfilling of the place and ministry to which God has called us in the Body have a deeper connection with our spiritual life than is generally recognized. To receive the Holy Spirit and the love of Christ into our hearts means death to every area of selfishness in our life. It means a complete surrender of our own interests as a member of the Body, so to give our life and love entirely to Christ and His Body. It means that the welfare of every member within our notice will become the supreme object of our desire. We need to realize what the Body of Christ is in reality—the vessel through which the blessed Spirit of God seeks to manifest himself.

59

We know what a masterpiece of divine workmanship a human body is, made from the dust, and yet the dwelling place and instrument in which the human soul can unfold and express itself. But this is but an image or a shadow of that Body of which Christ is the head. In regard to it our epistle tells us (1:22, 23) that God "gave Christ to be the head over all things to the church, which is his body, the fulness of him that filleth all in all." The Body of Christ is to contain and to exhibit the divine fullness as it dwells in Christ bodily. It tells us that "all the building fitly framed together groweth unto an holy temple in the Lord, in whom ye also are builded together for an habitation of God through the Spirit." It reminds us that "Christ loved the church and gave himself for it . . . that he might present it to himself a glorious church, not having spot, or wrinkle, or any such thing."

It suggests that all we know of the complex and integral union between our body members and our head, of the wonderful power that the head has to direct and use every member, and the readiness with which every member yields itself to the service of the head on behalf of its fellow members, is but a shadow of that still more mysterious union by which every believer is linked to Christ and ever holds himself at the disposal of his fellow believers.

"One Spirit and body." This Body of Christ is to be the highest revelation of the glory of God, manifesting His power to make the creature of the dust, fallen under the power of sin and Satan, into a partaker of the likeness and the holiness of the ever-blessed Son. It is this work over which the Holy Spirit presides in the individual believer to carry out the eternal purpose—that they all should be one, even as the Father is one with the Son. It is only as the Church yields herself to His divine working and His great purpose that the power of the Holy Spirit can be expected to work unhindered either in the Church as a whole or in the individual members.

The work which this Spirit of unity does is found in the following verses. When Christ ascended on high, He gave to His Church the gifts of apostles, prophets, evangelists, pastors and teachers "for the perfecting of the saints, for the work of ministry for the edifying of the body of Christ." Notice that it is not the apostles and prophets and pastors who are to build up the Body of Christ; their work is the perfecting or equipping of the saints for the saints' ministry of building up. Every saint is to be trained and equipped to do his part in the building up of the Body of Christ. Just as every member of my body helps the building up of the whole, so every believer is to know his place and work in the Body of Christ, caring for every other member. Each member needs the other; each member is to care for the others; each member is to feel himself so linked to the whole, in the love of the Spirit, that he will not only avoid and put away everything that is selfish or unloving, but will actively yield himself to the Spirit to be the instrument of God's edifying grace to all who are weaker.

We see the goal: "Till we all come in the unity of faith . . . unto a perfect man, unto the measure of the stature of the fulness of Christ." This is to be the goal of each member, not only for himself but for all around him, that the Body may be the fullness of God. With this attitude we can truly "grow up into him in all things, which is the head, even Christ; from whom the whole body fitly joined together and compacted . . . according to the effectual working in measure of every part, maketh increase of the body unto the edifying of itself in love."

The relationship of this to the spiritual life and our devotional life is clear. If our prayers only aim at our own perfection and happiness, they defeat themselves; the selfishness that is their goal prevents the answer. It is only in union with the whole Body that each member can be healthy and strong. The building up of the Body in love is indispensable to our spiritual health. Let us see to it that intercession, "with all prayer and supplication, praying at all seasons in the Spirit . . . for all the saints," be the proof that the Spirit of unity dwells and prays in us. Let us "love the brethren with a pure heart fervently." In our home life, in prayer circles, in all our fellowship with God's people, let our love watch over and encourage them, and ever remember that we are indispensable to each other. Let the Spirit of unity be the life of our private devotions; grace will be given to live our whole life in unceasing commitment to Christ and His glorious Body.

CHAPTER THIRTEEN
Grieving the Spirit

"Grieve not the holy Spirit of God" (Eph. 4:30).

We have a summary of the history of Israel and of the whole Old Testament covenant in the words of Isaiah: "They vexed his Holy Spirit"; and of Stephen: "Ye do always resist the Holy Ghost; as your fathers did, so do ye." The New Testament standard has shown that this should no longer be the case. God promised His people a new heart and a new spirit; a heart in which His law was written and into which He would put His Spirit. That indwelling Spirit would enable them to obey Him.

With the Spirit of God's Son living in us and having His reign over us, grieving our Father should no longer be a part of our lives. The warning, "Grieve not the Spirit," is also a promise; what grace commands it enables us to perform. The believer who desires to live unceasingly in the consciousness that he has been "sealed with the Holy Spirit" will find in his faith the assurance that the power and presence of that Spirit within him makes it possible to live without grieving Him.

And yet the danger is so near and so strong. Unless we live entirely under the power of the Spirit, we may not hear the warning. It is essential to make a study of all the possible hindrances to His work in us. The context (from v. 25) speaks of falsehood, anger, stealing, corrupt speech, and transgressions of the law of love. These were to be put far away; everything that is against God's law must grieve the Holy Spirit.

But there is more. Think of all the commands of the Lord Jesus as expressed through the Beatitudes concerning being poor in spirit, meek, merciful, and pure in heart; through all His teaching concerning bearing our cross, denying self, forsaking the world and following Him; down to His last commands to His disciples to love one another as He had loved them and to serve one another. These are some of the distinctive marks of the heavenly life Christ came to bring. Everything that is not in harmony with these must grieve the Spirit and prevent the enjoyment of His presence.

There is still more. When Paul tells us that "what is not of faith is sin," he reminds us how, while God's Word announces the great principles of our action, it leaves the individual believer under the teaching of the Spirit for the application of those principles in daily life. In little things, gray areas, in things regarding differences among Christians, the believer grieves the Spirit when he does not wait for His guidance or does not follow through on what appears to be the mind of the Spirit. Our whole life is to be under His control, with the heart watchful and ready to obey in everything. What is not of faith must be yielded up to God at once, or it may become the cloud that darkens the light of the Spirit in His divine tenderness.

Scripture speaks of the struggle between the flesh and the Spirit. It tells us that the only way in which a believer can live the life in the Spirit is through the power of the truth: "they that are of Christ Jesus have crucified the flesh." That means that even as Christ yielded His life and His flesh to the death of the cross, so the believer accepts

God's judgment on his whole sinful personality as embodied in the flesh. His own will, his own strength, his own goodness have been given up to the power of the Cross. He lives by the faith, "I am crucified with Christ, Christ liveth in me." Yielding to the flesh and allowing it to have its way must, by the very necessity of the case, hinder and grieve the blessed Spirit. Oh, what a tender, humble, watchful dependence upon the blessed Spirit and His leading is necessary if we are to maintain His undisturbed fellowship!

The great work of the Holy Spirit is to reveal Christ to the believer in the glory of His heavenly life and in the power by which He actually works in our hearts. As a preparation for this revelation, His first work is to convict of the sin of unbelief. The salvation God has prepared for us is totally comprised in Jesus Christ; the life He lived on earth, of humility and obedience, has been prepared for us and can be received through simple faith alone. The great secret to Christian living lies in this one thing: the daily, unceasing faith in who Jesus is and what He has for us. It roots in us the assurance that He will work in us every moment of our life. When this faith is not exercised or sought after, the Christian life will be totally ineffective. There is nothing that grieves the Holy Spirit more than the unbelief which prevents Jesus from displaying His power and His glory in working out His deliverance in our lives from the power of sin and of the world.

How desperately we need to see the simplicity and the glory of the Gospel we profess. In Jesus Christ there is stored up for us the new nature, all that by His life and death and resurrection He worked out. Out of this fullness of redemption we receive grace upon grace. He is the corn of wheat that died; the fullness of life that is in Christ is reproduced in us, enabling us to grow into the likeness of His humility and love and obedience. This is not by any power in ourselves. The Holy Spirit has been given and lives in us to communicate and maintain the life of Christ in the soul.

How urgent the command is: "Grieve not the Spirit of God!" May we not miss the unspeakable blessing that will come if we but yield to Him!

We are in search of the New Testament standard of a life of commitment. What does our text teach regarding Paul's thoughts about it? Could he have answered one of his readers asking about his experience, "I grieve and vex the Holy Spirit every day"? Surely not. And if he could not say this, would he have laid it down as the rule for others? Surely not. To any question he would have answered: "I am sure that the child of God, living fully in the power of the Holy Spirit, can please God; there is no necessity for grieving the Spirit every day."

Is the inferior standard of our modern Christianity the simple result of ignorance and unbelief in regard to the supernatural working of the ever-blessed Spirit in the heart? Paul lived his life of commitment in the fullness and the joy of the Holy Spirit. Is our standard limited by the fact that such a consistent experience is seldom taught and experienced? Is the cause that our knowledge is too much that of the intellect and that the Holy Spirit is not honored as the only teacher of spiritual truth? We need to return to the prayer in the first chapter (15-23), and what it teaches us of the absolute need of receiving from the Father the gift of the Spirit of wisdom. As the only teacher, the Holy Spirit alone can enable us to understand and experience the heavenly life that God has prepared for us.

CHAPTER FOURTEEN

Filled with the Spirit

"Be not drunk with wine ... but be filled with the Spirit; speaking to yourselves in psalms and hymns and spiritual songs" (Eph. 5:18, 19).

"Grieve not the Spirit!" "Be filled with the Spirit!" These two commands encompass all of our responsibility to the Spirit. The one is negative—warning against anything of the flesh or self that would lead to unbelief or disobedience to Christ Jesus. The other is positive—calling us to commit our whole personality in undivided surrender to the Father who reveals and maintains the life of Christ within us.

To understand the command, "Be filled with the Spirit," we only need to turn to the day of Pentecost when the disciples were "filled with the Holy Spirit." From the account we know what that meant to them. For three years they had lived day and night in close fellowship with the Lord. His presence had been everything to them. When He spoke about His departure, their hearts were troubled. He promised that the Spirit would come; not to take His place, but to reveal himself as their Lord. Through the Spirit He would be ever present with them as much as when He was upon earth, only in a far more intimate and glorious way.

He would no longer simply be near them and beside them, without the power to enable them to do what He had taught them. He would live and work in them, even as the Father had lived and worked in Him as a man. To be filled with the Spirit meant that Christ on the throne would be to them an ever-present, living reality, filling their hearts and life with all His heavenly love and joy. Their past fellowship with Him during His earthly ministry would prove to have been but the shadow of that intense and unceasing union with Him, which the Spirit would reveal in power.

The command, "Be filled with the Spirit," is a promise that what the disciples received and enjoyed at Pentecost is, indeed, for us, too. The Church has existed at a level far inferior to the life of Pentecost. The spirit of the world and of human wisdom is far too prevalent. Few believe in the possibility of the unbroken presence of Christ dwelling in the heart; conquering sin by His holy presence, inspiring to commitment and perfect self-sacrifice by the fire of His love, guiding each day into all His will by the leading of His Spirit. The heavenly vision of Christ at the right hand of God ministering in the power of His infinite redemption is extremely rare. His redemptive ministry includes not only salvation to those who repent, but full salvation to all whom He has sanctified by His one offering. As the result, there are but few in the Church who witness to "the exceeding greatness of his power to us-ward who believe."

The condition for receiving this blessing is best seen in the account concerning the disciples. They had turned their back upon the world and forsaken all to follow Christ. They had come to know and love Him and to do His will. As our Savior said, "If ye love me, ye will keep my commandments, and I will pray the Father, and he will give you another Comforter." They had continued with Him in His temptations; He carried them with Him through death and the grave; the joy and the power of the resurrection life filled their hearts with confidence and hope. Their whole being was committed and, one might say, lost in the ascended Lord upon the throne—they were indeed ready, fully prepared to receive the wondrous gift that was to come upon them.

The Church of our day is sadly lacking in that same separation from the world and that corresponding intense attachment and obedience to Christ. Fellowship with His suffering and conformity to His death are only bywords. Devotion to Christ on the throne and the confident expectation of the never-ceasing flow of the water of life from under that throne are all but nonexistent in the Church. Is it any wonder that the power of God is so little known and experienced in our church life!

Turn once again to Pentecost and consider the wondrous gift that was bestowed upon the Church. Though they did not immediately know what it meant, the Spirit awakened the consciousness that He, by whom the Son and the Father had come to dwell in them, was himself the true God. He was the overflowing fountain, from whom rivers of life would flow in them and from them into the world. Coming directly from the throne of heaven, He rested upon them as the Spirit of glory and of God and filled their hearts with the very love and power of Christ in glory. As the mighty power of God dwelling in them, He convinced the world by their boldness and by their love that God was indeed in their midst.

How different this is from the conception that most Christians have of the Spirit. How different this is from today's experience of the presence and the power that He imparts. The thought of the Holy Spirit is little more than a mental conception or a passing emotion, with its sense of power or of happiness. How little there is of the consciousness that fills the soul with deep reverence and quiet rest, with heavenly joy and strength, as the natural and permanent possession of the life of the believer. The name of the Holy Spirit, twelve times repeated in our epistle, in His many graces is to mark the character of the life of the Church just as He did in the New Testament Church.

"Be filled with the Spirit." This filling has its differences in degrees. There is the first joy of a new convert in a revival; then onward, through all the experiences by which he is taught what more is needed and is waiting for him. So, he will be filled with all the fullness of God that comes through the dwelling of Christ in the heart.

Two things are needed in the filling of a water glass. First, the glass must be clean, empty and ready, even in its posture, to receive the water that is waiting for it. Second, the water must be near and ready to empty itself in full measure into the waiting glass. In the transaction between God and man for the filling of the Spirit, man must first know the completeness of the surrender that is needed, and that, even to the death of self and the world, the commitment of the whole personality is indispensable. And then man needs to know how willing and ready the Holy God is to take possession of our being and to fill it with himself.

When our Lord Jesus said, "He that believeth on me, out of him shall flow rivers of living water," He made the one condition of being filled with the Spirit that of simple faith in Jesus himself. Faith is not imagination, not argument nor intellectual conviction; it claims the whole heart, it commits the whole personality; it entrusts itself unreservedly to the power that seeks to take possession of it. It is in this life of faith, cultivated in private devotion and adoring worship, in unceasing dependence and wholehearted surrender, that the blessing will be found.

We need to carefully evaluate our present commitment of heart to God. We need to call upon our blessed Lord to deliver us from all that would hinder us from a life of full faith and close fellowship with himself. We are called to worship and to wait until God the Spirit dwells within us, revealing the Father and the Son and all that wonderful life of heaven whereby He works in the heart as He does in heaven above.

CHAPTER FIFTEEN

The Sword of the Spirit

"Take the sword of the Spirit, which is the word of God" (Eph. 6:17).

Paul begins the last section of the epistle with the words, "Finally, . . . be strong in the Lord, and in the power of his might." In 1:19 he had written of "the exceeding greatness of his power to us-ward who believe"—the resurrection power by which Christ was lifted to the throne. In 3:16 he had spoken of our "being strengthened with might by his Spirit in the inner man"—the divine power which is to be the normal experience of these believers. They are to prove in and through their lives that God's power as manifested in His Church is a divine reality.

The Holy Spirit is the mighty power of God. The Spirit-filled Christian is to be strengthened and equipped for God's service and the spiritual warfare regarding God's Kingdom. He warns them that they "wrestle not against flesh and blood, but against principalities, against powers, against the rulers of the darkness of this world, against spiritual wickedness in high places." It is crucial for them to live every day clothed in the whole armor of God, standing strong in Christ and in the strength of His might. The believer not only has to meet the evil spirits that tempt him, but he also has to regard himself as a soldier in the army that Christ leads to warfare against the kingdom of darkness in all its forms. In the warfare of the Church, the victory of the Cross over the power of Satan is to be carried out in the same power through which Christ triumphed over the grave.

When Paul says, "Put on the whole armour of God," he begins by defining the various parts of the defense. The Christian needs to realize that his entire personality is defended in the protection of his Lord. Properly defended, he is always ready to take action on the offensive. Paul mentions only one offensive weapon—the sword. That sword is the sword of the Spirit, the Word of God.

To know its power and how to use it effectively, we need only look to our leader, the captain of the Lord's host. When Jesus Christ met Satan in the wilderness, He conquered him by the Word of God alone. He had studied that Word, loved it, obeyed it, and had lived in it. The Holy Spirit found in Him the familiar words with which He could meet and conquer every satanic suggestion. To take the sword of the Spirit in the hour of battle means that I have lived in that Word and have it abiding in me; that I have lived it out, and have it as the master of my personality.

The Spirit of Christ within me enables the power of my faith to cast away Satan by the Word of God. It is the man who commits his entire personality to the Word of God, who "lives by every word that proceedeth out of the mouth of God," who will be a good soldier of Jesus Christ. Whether in the struggle with worldliness, with open sin or hidden iniquity, with feeble faith, with dark superstition, with nominal Christianity, with a backsliding church, or with the kingdom of darkness—the Word of God will always and everywhere be the weapon of victory for those who know how to use it correctly.

Who know how to use it correctly! We learn what that means from the vision of John when he saw One like the

Son of Man, and "out of his mouth went a sharp two-edged sword" (Rev. 1:16). Later, John heard Him speak, "These things saith he which hath the sharp sword with two edges. . . . Repent, or else I will come unto thee quickly, and will fight against them with the sword of my mouth" (Rev. 2:12, 16). When Christ has been revealed to us, calling us to repent of every sin, and above all, of the sin of our unbelief, and has warred against us and the evil in us with the sword of His mouth, the power of the Word will be revealed in us, and we shall be strong to wield it as the sword of the Spirit.

Hebrews 4:12 shows the effectiveness of God's Word: "For the word of God is quick, and powerful, and sharper than any two-edged sword, piercing even to the dividing asunder of soul and spirit" (showing on the one hand all that is soulish or natural, and that which is spiritual and divine). It is the "discerner of the thoughts and intents of the heart," discovering our most secret intentions and inclinations in the light of God and His holiness. It is the branch that has been pruned through the Word that will bear much fruit. Only the soul that has fully yielded itself to the sword of His mouth will have faith and strength to wield it against every enemy.

Every believer is to be a soldier in Christ's army. The spiritual powers of darkness are to be met and overcome by all who have been made partakers of the divine nature. They are not to live for themselves, but wholly for Him who bought them. From heaven He leads them as His conquering hosts, to rout the spiritual hosts of wickedness in heavenly places. What a wonder that so many Christians have never understood their calling and have never given their lives unreservedly for the one object of securing the triumph of our Redeemer in the world!

Let us listen to the declaration that calls us to the war! Let us confess and repent that we have so seldom stood in the strength of the Lord and in the power of His might! Let our ears listen to the call that comes from every church for men and women who will yield themselves to Christ for His service, whether at home or the foreign field!

We must remember that it is in our own life that we are to prove the power of God's Word in prayer and intercession, and with ourselves in surrender and cleansing. It is there we learn to use it. It is there that the love for our Lord and the love for souls will awaken us to the war. It is there that the Word of God will in reality become the sword of the Spirit, that we will always carry it secured on our thigh, ready to meet the enemy and to deliver his captives.

How helpless in comparison is the Church of our day! Its meager missionary force is hardly prepared to meet the needs of the billions who have yet to hear the name of Jesus. Yet, how strong it might be if every believer were to be trained to yield himself to the sharp two-edged sword proceeding out of the mouth of the Son of Man. When the Word of God has done its work in our lives, we will have power to grasp it and to carry its deliverance to those who are dying in satanic bondage.

God forgive us that our devotional life has so often been the vain attempt to find nourishment or joy in the Word of God. We failed because our first thought was that of seeking comfort or holiness for ourselves. We need to learn that a Christian has been brought to Christ that Christ may use him as a member of His Body for the welfare of the whole. That would include those who have not yet been gathered into it. Our devotions should bear these two marks: the entire surrender to the Word of God as the two-edged sword, dividing soul and spirit; the surrender to wield that two-edged sword in the faith of the power of God's Holy Spirit against every enemy of Christ and His Kingdom. Light and blessing will flow into hours of devotion when we meet those conditions.

CHAPTER SIXTEEN

The Spirit of Prayer

"Praying always with all prayer and supplication, in the Spirit, and watching thereunto with all perseverance and supplication for all saints; and for me . . ." (Eph. 6:18, 19).

These words are connected with the preceding context: Be strong in the Lord, put on the whole armor of God. Our battle is against the spiritual hosts of wickedness in the heavenly places. Stand, therefore, putting on the whole armor of God, both defensive and offensive, with all prayer and supplication, praying at all times in the Spirit. The Christian's power, the Christian's wrestling, his putting on the armor, and his wielding the sword of the Spirit is all to be in unceasing dependence upon God. It cannot be accomplished apart from the believing confidence in His all-sufficient grace. A life of unceasing prayer is the secret of a life of victory. Praying always in the Spirit is the mark of a normal spiritual life.

This praying at all times is to be in relationship with the Holy Spirit. As unceasingly as my lungs are kept breathing and my heart beating by the divine power which upholds my physical life, the Holy Spirit must continually breathe in me that prayer life by which the powers of the divine life and the heavenly world are maintained. Salvation is not by works, or effort, or struggling. I am God's workmanship, created in Christ Jesus for good works which God declares are already prepared that we should walk in them. Being a divine creation we are not left to ourselves, but are moment by moment upheld by the Word of His power. Unceasing prayer is possible, is commanded, because the eternal Spirit ever maintains it as the spiritual breathing of the soul.

This praying at all times is never to be selfish in nature, with its reference only to our own needs: "Watching thereunto with all perseverance and supplication for all the saints." In the epistle Paul has taught the importance of the truth of the unity of the Body of Christ in love (2:13-22; 3:16, 18; 4:1-16; 5:22-33). As he has spoken of the battling to which believers are called with the powers of darkness, he speaks here of the unity of the saints as forming one great army as the host of the Lord, living by one Spirit, and all striving together for the establishment of His kingdom in the world. Continual prayer for all believers is not only the duty of each member; it is the essential factor upon which the welfare and the victory of the whole depends.

We can learn from Paul's own petitions what we are to pray for concerning the saints. Look back to Ephesians 1:15-23 and its prayer on behalf of those who had already been sealed with the Spirit. Paul asked that God would give them the Spirit of wisdom and divine understanding that they might know the exceeding greatness of His power in all who believe. Oh, how believers need this great truth to secure a place in their hearts and thoroughly empower them! How believers who have received this need to be reminded of their calling to pray for those who have not received it. The health of the Church as a whole, the spiritual strength of individual believers or churches, depends upon unceasing prayer in all perseverance and supplication for all the saints.

We must, also, study the prayer in 3:14-21 where Paul

bows his knees and cries that God might grant something special "according to the riches of his glory." He desired that the believers might be strengthened with divine power so that they may be filled with all the fullness of God. Stop and meditate on this thought. True believers stand greatly in need of the prayers of all to whom the Spirit of supplication is given. The prayer is to be definite: pleading for the Spirit of divine power to fill their whole inner man, that Christ may dwell in their hearts, and they be rooted in love. All believers are to unite in prayer that God will bring into reality this strength for every believer.

Such prayer is to be in continual devotion to God. Prayer always in the Spirit for all saints will be the secret of true revival in God's children. "And on my behalf!" The minister who is praying as an intercessor for the saints whom he cares for has equal need of their prayers in return. As the lifeblood, which is ever purified by the fresh air we breathe, circulates through the whole body and maintains its unity in vital power, even so the Spirit of prayer is essential to the health of every member of the Body of Christ. The spirit of prayer is continually breathing in the atmosphere of heaven and breathing up to heaven the unceasing petitions of love on behalf of the whole Body and every member.

The work of the ministry depends upon unceasing prayer. The minister is to train believers to pray like this as one of their highest privileges. The work of the missionary who, like Paul, carries the Gospel to the lost, depends upon it. If we truly believed in the power that could come upon our missionaries in answer to unceasing prayer in their behalf, what grace would come in answer! The power "to make known with boldness the mystery of the gospel" would come upon their preaching. To the wise or to the ignorant, to the Greek or the Jew, to the follower of Mohammed or of idols, Christ would be effectively declared as the power of God and the wisdom of God.

In our devotional life, we need a vision of the work to be done. A vision of the hosts of spiritual wickedness in heavenly places, of Jesus Christ exalted over all and carrying out the triumph of the Cross, and of ministers and members of Christ laboring together and battling in preaching and in praying for the conquest of the world. Oh, what a new meaning and purpose our devotions would have! This is life in the Spirit as He has been revealed in this epistle, a life strong in the Lord and the exceeding greatness of His strength within us. We no longer live to ourselves and our selfish religious hopes and efforts, but we live in love, even as Christ loved us. Each must give himself as a sacrifice and an offering to God for the building up of the Body of Christ.

May God help us to glimpse the inspiration of the true standard of life that the epistle has held out to us. We need an undoubting confidence that God will make this life a reality, even a life of unceasing prayer in the Spirit for all the saints.

CHAPTER SEVENTEEN

Ephesians in Review

"Who [God] hath blessed us with all spiritual blessings in heavenly places in Christ" (Eph. 1:3).

In our epistle the expression "the heavenly places" is used five times. "In heavenly places," God has blessed us with every spiritual blessing in Christ; He has set Christ at His own right hand; He has made us sit with Christ; the manifold wisdom of God is to be made known through the Church to the principalities and powers; we are to be equipped for battling the spiritual hosts of wickedness. The life of the Christian is regarded in this spiritual and heavenly aspect; it can be lived only in the power of the heavenly world.

The Epistle to the Ephesians has been called "The Alps of the New Testament." As one peak rises above another, so the Apostle leads us through the heavenly truths of election and redemption, of the mystery of God's will and His purpose in Christ, of our resurrection and ascension with Christ, our new creation and all the glory of the Body of Christ. As the light of the Holy Spirit shines upon one truth after another, we discern how truly divine and heavenly our life on earth is meant to be.

We have studied the twelve passages in which the Holy Spirit is mentioned. Our purpose here is to gather all their teaching into one, and see if we accurately picture the man called to live by this heavenly standard:

1. The sealing of the Spirit. The believer has been sealed in Christ by the Holy Spirit of promise, the down payment of his inheritance. The Holy Spirit is the guarantee of what the believer can become in Christ, the divine assurance that every promise can be made true. He has the seal of God upon his forehead; his personality bears the stamp of the Holy Spirit.

2. The first great work of the Spirit is that He opens our understanding to know what we have been called to by God and to what the exceeding greatness of God's power is to enable us to live worthy of that calling. The Holy Spirit reveals the working of God's power in raising Christ from the dead to the throne of glory as the guarantee of what God will daily work in us.

3. The believer, brought near by the blood, lives in the Holy Place, lives through the Spirit a life of abiding access to God in Christ Jesus.

4. The believer no longer lives for himself. As a member of the great spiritual temple built for a dwelling place of God through the Spirit, he is linked to the chief cornerstone and to all his fellow saints by the Spirit.

5. The believer knows the mystery of Christ among the Gentiles and counts them as fellow heirs to whom all the unsearchable riches of Christ are to be made known. He lives for the Kingdom and the ingathering of the lost as Christ's inheritance.

6. The believer learns that it is only by an almighty power that he can live his life in the heavenly places. His continual prayer is that the power of the Spirit may strengthen him mightily, that Christ may dwell in his heart by faith, and that he with all the saints may be filled with love and with all the fullness of God. He asks for himself

and for others that God in His infinite power may reveal His Son in them.

7. The believer bears the mark of the likeness of Jesus, the meek and lowly One. He walks worthy of his heavenly calling, in all lowliness and meekness, maintaining the unity of the Spirit. He knows that he can do this because God strengthens him with might in the inner man.

8. The believer knows that there is one body and one spirit. His one calling is to live for the work of ministering to the saints in building up the Body of Christ in love.

9. The believer seeks above everything else never to grieve the Holy Spirit. How dare he break the seal that God has set upon him, the Spirit of a holy life? It is only in a life of holiness that he can partake of all the blessings in the heavenly places in Christ. He cultivates a tender spirit.

10. "Be filled with the Spirit." The more the believer knows the blessedness of the Spirit and all the work that He does, the more intense the desire awakens to yield himself in utter surrender to His control. At the same time he senses the need of a deeper vision of the riches of that grace which the Spirit is given to pour out. He sees that to be filled with the Spirit means peace and joy and righteousness.

11. The sealing of the Spirit includes the calling to be a soldier and to be strong in the Lord and the power of His might. The believer begins to understand why such divine power is promised him. Armed with the sword of the Spirit he will battle the powers of evil and rescue men for Christ and His service.

12. The believer knows to obey the call to a life of continual prayer, watching with all perseverance for all saints and for all ministers of the Word. The Spirit makes it possible for them to be true soldiers and prayer warriors.

"Blessed be the God and Father of our Lord Jesus Christ, who hath blessed us with all spiritual blessings in heavenly places in Christ!" We need to meditate on the twelvefold blessing until we realize what a salvation God has prepared for us. A believer is to be sealed by the Spirit; taught by the Spirit to know the divine power working in him; kept in the full consciousness of an abiding access to the Father; united with all his fellow saints in the one temple as the dwelling place of God; led into the mystery of Christ among the Gentiles; strengthened with power by the Spirit in the inner man to have Christ dwelling in the heart; and to be filled with all the fullness of God.

Coming down into his everyday life, the believer is to walk in all meekness and lowliness; keep the unity of the Spirit; minister in the power of the Spirit for the building up of the Body in love; seek to never grieve the Spirit; be filled with the Spirit; fulfill the law of love in all his daily life; be strong in the Lord and the power of His might to fulfill his destiny in wrestling with the powers of darkness in the use of the Word and prayer for all saints.

We need time, thought, prayer, and quiet waiting on the Spirit of God to see this vision and to maintain it. The Spirit-sealed, Spirit-taught, Spirit-strengthened, Spirit-filled life as described is to be the normal spiritual experience. We need to turn away from self and the world and to allow God to work in us all His purpose according to the counsel of His own will.

Let us not forget the purpose with which we began the study of the epistle. Let us believe in the divine standard of the Christian life it sets before us. Let us believe in the almighty power of God by which it can become ours. Let us believe that if we are sincere in seeking deliverance from an inferior standard, we can count upon the infinite mercy of God to work in us what otherwise appears to be utterly hopeless—a life filled with the Spirit.

CHAPTER EIGHTEEN
Because of Unbelief

"Why could not we cast him out? And Jesus said unto them, Because of your unbelief" (Matt. 17:19, 20).

In connection with our last chapter, I wish that it were possible to ask my readers whether they think it possible to carry out the Ephesian standard of the spiritual life in their own daily practice. Many might answer that though, to a man like Paul and those whom he calls spiritual men, such a standard is possible, it is not within reach of all; such a life is not for them. A large majority are content to think of it as an attractive ideal, which, though not within our reach, exercises its stimulating and elevating influence even on those who remain far below it.

Yet, the more I study the epistle, the deeper the convictions grows: Paul meant in all sincerity to declare what God had not only shown by revelation, but had actually worked within him. He speaks in chapter one not only of the revelation of the Spirit to make us know "the exceeding greatness of [God's] power," but in chapter three of our being "strengthened with might by his spirit in the inner man," so that the great miracle of grace might be perfected in us: Christ dwelling in the heart, filling us with all the fullness of God. When he adds the ascription of praise, "Now unto him that is able to do exceeding abundantly above all that we ask or think, according to the power that worketh in us, unto him be glory in the church," he undoubtedly means that this was his own experience and he confidently urges his readers to believe that it can be theirs. The exceeding greatness of God's power working in the heart from moment to moment, day by day, is the ground on which the standard of commitment rests, which he holds out to us. But this commitment needs unceasing prayer to know this power, to believe it, to receive it—Paul's two great prayers show this. Without this power, the standard is an impossible one; with this power, it is seen as within our reach.

The question must be asked: How is it that in the Church this mighty power of God working in us is so seldom taught and experienced? Is the whole Church in error as it rests content with a far lower standard than what this epistle holds out to us? The answer to this question will lead us to the discovery of the root problem from which the Church is suffering.

We know that God set Abraham before Israel as the great example of faith in Him, believing that God was able to give life to the dead, both in his own case and in the sacrifice of Isaac. Yet, we know how Israel, from the very commencement of God's dealings in Egypt, continually grieved Him by unbelief until at length it was condemned to forty years' wanderings in the wilderness. And onward through those years, as Psalm 78 tells us, "they turned back and tempted God, and limited the Holy One of Israel."

We know, too, how our Lord Jesus continually sought to cultivate in His disciples the habit of faith as the one condition for their seeing the power and the glory of God. When He commissioned Paul as the last of the apostles, Paul was used as a witness to the power of faith, not only in justification, but in the entirety of spiritual life and service. And, yet, just as Israel utterly failed in believing God, so in the

Church it became evident from the beginning just how little man understands concerning salvation through trust in God alone. We know how utterly the Galatians failed; how sternly the Epistle to the Hebrews warns about unbelief; and how quickly the Church of the second century was brought into bondage under a system of law. The entire history of the Church is a proof of how naturally the human heart turns from grace and faith to law and works.

In the lives of the Church Fathers we find, despite all their earnestness, how little they understood of faith in the power of God as the one secret of spiritual life. The result was the cultivating of a religion in which the grace of God was always connected with the confession of much sinning, while the tone of Paul and his faith in God's mighty keeping and saving power was seldom heard. The generations to which the Reformation brought the gospel of justification by faith found it difficult to understand that sanctification is as much by faith. Few believers discovered that the power of a holy life for victory over the world and the flesh is only found in an immediate and unceasing exercise of faith in the exceeding greatness of God's power working in us. Is it any surprise, then, that the Church of our day is still bound in unbelief in the mighty power of Jesus?

We often hear complaints of the lack of power in the Church, both to guide its members to a true commitment to Christ and the service of His kingdom and to influence the unsaved masses around us. Many causes are mentioned, but the chief cause is seldom understood: a Church that does not experience and declare the power of Christ dwelling in the hearts of His people to overcome the power of sin cannot expect that mighty power in its battle with Satan and his hosts. The first great work of the Holy Spirit is to unmask our unbelief. When that work of conviction is incomplete, the Church will be helpless to do its work. The Church must be brought to confess that its feebleness is due to one thing: its not giving Christ His place of honor. "All power in heaven and on earth is given to me." As the Church believes and experiences this, she will learn to expect Him to do His might works.

Let me once again urge every reader to ask himself the question: Do I believe in the power of God in Christ to work in me the life depicted in this epistle? Instead of mourning over the sins that we cannot master, the pride, the self-will, the lack of love, the shortcoming in obedience to all God's will, let us come to the root of the problem and confess the terrible sin of our unbelief in "the exceeding greatness of [God's] power" revealed in Christ and in the "strengthening by the Spirit with might" which leads us on to the fullness of God. As we commit ourselves to the Holy Spirit in the confession of our unbelief, He has promised to powerfully reveal Christ in us so that our life can indeed become the response to the divine call: "Be strong in the Lord and in the power of his might."

CHAPTER NINETEEN

Possible with God

"Who then can be saved? And he said, The things which are impossible with men are possible with God" (Luke 18:26, 27).

If the great hindrance to the power of God's Spirit working in our lives is the thought, "the standard is an impossible one," our only hope is to listen to the voice of Christ when He tells us that what is impossible with man is possible to God. God can do for us what appears to be utterly beyond our reach. God by His Spirit desires to work in us all that He worked in Paul. We have this written confidence that He will do it for us. Let us think what is implied in the great gift of the Holy Spirit.

Few words are used with such a variety of meanings as the word "spirit." Its meanings range from anything in which the mind of man exerts and proves its power to the very highest revelation of God's holiness and love. The same word "spirit" is used in so many ways that it is exposed to the danger of everyone understanding it according to his own point of view. Within the sphere of Bible truth we often suffer from a very partial and defective view of what is meant by the Spirit of God and of Christ. We need to realize what God means when He promises us the Spirit of Christ.

When Jesus Christ came into the world as a full human being, He purposed by His life to obey His Father in perfect holiness and love; it is this same life that God means to impart to those who believe in Christ. When Christ died, it was that He might lay down His life and then, just as the grain of wheat dies and reappears in the full head of wheat with its hundredfold reproduction of the seed, live again in our lives here upon earth. The Father gave Him for this purpose. When He ascended to the throne, the Spirit was poured out as His own life into the heart of His people. "God gave us the spirit of his Son, crying, Abba, Father." The Spirit communicates the holiness and disposition of Christ with a divine power to all who believe, and that in proportion to how much they believe. They live by the Spirit and are led by the Spirit; the Spirit is their life.

In the wondrous union of the divine and the human life in the believer, everything depends on the relationship that is being maintained. God must be working the all in all, and man must be receiving all from God to work it out in trust and obedience. When this is not understood, man is always pushing in with his own efforts and taking the role that God himself would fill. Man thinks that if by sincere prayer he can secure God's help in his efforts, he has found the path to holiness and to growth. He does not understand that the role of the Spirit must be one of absolute and entire control and his own place that of direct and unceasing dependence. This can be seen when two men may be praying that God would give them the Spirit of wisdom or of power. One may be thinking only of the limited help that he has always connected with the thought of the Spirit, while the other is expecting that God will do for him above what he can ask or think.

The great secret of the Christian life is found in that death to the self-life, in that being brought to death by the cross of Christ, in which the power of Christ's death manifests itself in us. We know how our Lord Jesus had to give up the life He had lived upon earth in order to impart His life to His people. He had to take His place among the dead in utter weakness and helplessness before He could live again by the power of God. His death on the cross was indispensable to the life of the Spirit. And as it was with Christ, so it must be with us. As we yield ourselves to be united with Him in His death, we can share with Him in the glory and power of the life of the Spirit. To know what the Holy Spirit means implies the knowing of what death means. The work of the Cross and the Spirit are inseparable. The soul that understands that death to the self-life is the gate to true life is on the path to learning what and who the Holy Spirit is.

The low standard of what the Holy Spirit can and will do for us is evident in our churches. The distinctive mark of the Apostolic Church was the presence of the Holy Spirit in power; the distinctive mark of the Church today is the lack of power in the Spirit. Our conversions, our preaching, our fellowship, our life, our work for God and His Kingdom—all are characterized by a severe lack of power.

There are endless discussions and efforts being carried on to attempt to lift our churches to a higher level and to bring the masses to acknowledge and accept the truth of God's Word. There has not been, however, on the part of the Church as a whole anything like what is truly needed. Change will come only with the intense and repentant confession that as churches and Christians, we have grieved the Spirit of God. Yes, you and I, whose calling it is to honor Him and to prove by His presence in our life that Christ is indeed Lord of all.

In the Epistle to the Ephesians the Holy Spirit occupies a prominent place. Paul has a specific reason for writing and saturating the entire epistle with the truth of the Spirit's presence and work. The Epistle to the Colossians was written about the same time and bears many similarities concerning the state of Paul's mind. And, yet, there is one marked difference. In Colossians the Holy Spirit is mentioned only once; in Ephesians, twelve times. It is as though he felt the need for giving expression to a system of truth in which the presence and power of the Holy Spirit in the life of the Christian should be specifically set forth. Think of what we would have missed if the epistle were lacking this preoccupation with the person and power of the Holy Spirit! Let us thank God for the gift, and seek to link the truth of the spiritual blessings to the living Spirit, through whom they all come.

We need to make sure that when we think of the Holy Spirit we mean what God means. He means the Holy Spirit, God the Spirit, God the Holy One, God in His holiness living within us. The more we yield ourselves to this thought, the clearer we will understand these two great truths. First, we need to understand that in the Holy Spirit we encounter the whole of God, not only His power, but the living God himself. Second, we need to understand that the whole man—spirit, soul and body—needs to be controlled by Him. As these two truths work into our lives and we think of what God in the Spirit is willing to do in us, we will be convinced that nothing can keep Him from doing His work in us except something in ourselves. We will know that our great need is to die with Christ to the self-life so that the new life brought to life in Christ may be the proper dwelling place for all the blessing the presence of the Spirit will bring.

CHAPTER TWENTY
Unto Him Be Glory

"Now unto him that is able to do exceeding abundantly above all that we ask or think, according to the power that worketh in us, unto him be glory" (Eph. 3:20, 21).

There is still one point which I have not pressed as strongly as I should have. It is the place which the power of God takes in the epistle and is meant to take in the life of the Christian. The reader must be brought to realize that all we have learned about the Holy Spirit cannot have its full effect without a very special and entire surrender to the almighty working of God's power. This surrender must be accompanied by a very intense, personal and abiding faith that that power must be known and honored as the one secret of a life that will measure up to the New Testament standard. Only God can give us the understanding of His Spirit to know "the exceeding greatness of his power to usward who believe."

It is remarkable what prominence Paul gives to the thought of our entire salvation being under the working of God's almighty power. In 1:11, he speaks of "the purpose of him who worketh all things after the counsel of his own will." God does this, not only regarding the great work of

deliverance through Christ, but equally in every detail of
the daily life of the Christian. We too often think of Him as
the omnipotent One, able to work mightily where He sees
the need. But the words suggest something far greater; He
is the God who works unceasingly, every moment, not only
in nature with its every leaf and flower, but in His children,
too. He works all that they need for carrying out His blessed
will.

The reader knows the words in the prayer in chapter
one: "The exceeding greatness of his power to us-ward who
believe." Paul teaches his readers that the power of His
might that raised Christ from the dead is sufficient for the
daily need of your soul, and can effect and carry out in you
what God has purposed and longs to see in you. It is only as
the Holy Spirit brings you the spiritual insight into this
power and enables you to carry it about with you as the ha-
bitual consciousness of what God is working in you that God
will be able to do for you beyond all you have asked or
thought.

The normal pattern in the Christian life is to strive after
the standard that the Word sets before us, with the prayer
that God will help us in our weakness. This pattern completely misses "the exceeding greatness of [God's] power"
that alone can do the work in us. "The weakness of God is
stronger than man." The strength of God is to be found only
in the consciousness of our own utter weakness. This was
the mark of the working of His power in Christ. Our Lord
died, sinking down into absolute weakness, without an
ounce of the power of thought or of will. He yielded himself
utterly to the Father, and God's power raised Him out of
that absolute weakness to the place of power on the throne.
Only the teaching of the Holy Spirit can enable us to know
this exceeding greatness of God's power working in us.

This thought must master us if we would understand
the standard of life that Paul puts before us. It is the
thought of what God will work in us that will give us the

courage to see and to accept a life that pleases Him in everything.

In 3:7, Paul speaks of the grace of God given him "by the effectual working of his power." He appears to have experienced and to have counted upon this direct working of God in all the grace he needed for his ministry. He adds in Colossians: "I labor, striving according to his working, which worketh in me mightily." The man who believes this principle of faith will cease from striving for power in himself; his whole attitude will be that of simple dependence and perfect trust.

At the close of chapter three Paul returns to the thought of God's almighty power. In chapter one he had spoken of the Spirit's enlightenment to show us that the power that raised Christ is needed to work in us in every moment and every action of our spiritual life. In chapter three he goes further and prays that the exceeding greatness of God's power, "according to the riches of his glory"—oh, to take time and think what that means!—may be given us as an actual strengthening with power by His Spirit in the inner man. That can only mean that the whole spiritual life be permanently brought to life with such divine power that the indwelling of Christ in the heart—personal, conscious and abiding—will be a divine reality. The Church has nearly lost the thought of the indwelling of Christ as a continual experience. Before this can become a reality in our faith and experience, we must learn to count upon the exceeding greatness of God's power as a part of the inheritance of every Christian, of which the Holy Spirit is the down payment.

To show how full Paul's mind was of the thought of the divine power as the one condition of the spiritual life, the doxology which he adds gives God glory for this one thing—that He is able to do, not only what has just been spoken of, but "exceeding abundantly above all that we ask or think." There are other attributes of God—His love, His righteousness, His holiness—for which we bless His name. But we need to be reminded that His almighty power must always be our one confidence for all that He is to do in us in carrying out His purpose. Let us take time to worship and adore—"Now unto him be glory"—until every thought of what is to be done in us, and in the Church, and in the world is summed up in one statement of faith: "Able to do exceeding abundantly above all that we ask or think, according to the power that worketh in us!"

Just one more word. In his last section (6:10), Paul closes all his instruction in the epistle with the conclusion: "Finally, my brethren, be strong in the Lord, and in the power of his might." This is the same word which he had used concerning the raising of Christ (1:19), "according to the working of his mighty power"; and (3:16) "to be strengthened with might by his Spirit in the inner man." That was meant to be the standard of commitment in the Ephesian Christians. That will become the standard of our commitment when we learn to cast all our weakness at His feet and begin to believe with childlike confidence and assurance in the exceeding greatness of His power toward us. Then we will be equipped for a life strong in the Lord and in the power of His might.

Notes

CHAPTER SIX

1. "But I thought that they had the Spirit already! Yes, certainly; but here is a further gift of the Spirit, a deeper draught. The blessed stream of the Holy Ghost is forever proceeding from the Father and the Son. There is no finality in this work. It is not like Christ's work—a finished work. Observe that there is no expression in Scripture which limits the power or the measure of the outgoing of the Holy Ghost. There is no word to say that the Spirit of God is come to an individual or a church, and that therefore the door may be shut because there is no more Spirit of God to come. We are to be ever receiving, and ever expending, and yet ever expecting at the same time. We must be for evermore opening our hearts to receive further gifts and provisions, for ever letting in great waves of the Spirit to pour through our life. May our God flood us all afresh with fuller waves of truth, and love, and power."—Rev. C. A. Fox, *The Spiritual Grasp of the Epistles.*

2. The Spirit was needed to give a fuller knowledge of God himself. The word used in the Greek implies intimate spiritual apprehension. Then follow three great things into which spiritual insight is needed for the Christian life:

(1) The hope of His calling—the knowledge of the hope

95

which God held out to them when He called them. In verse four Paul had said, "He chose us that we should be holy and without blame before him in love." What light shines upon these words when the Holy Spirit shows us the possibilities they imply and how God himself will make them true in us.

(2) "What the riches of the glory of his inheritance in the saints." There is a twofold inheritance. We are God's heritage. It is of this we read in verse 11, "In whom also we have obtained an inheritance." And God is our heritage. Of this we read in verse 14, "The Holy Spirit is an earnest of our inheritance." "The riches of the glory of his inheritance in the saints," which the Holy Spirit is to reveal, includes both. The words in Colossians (1:27) show us that this means Christ in us, "the riches of the glory of this mystery, which is Christ in you, the hope of glory." Christ is God's treasure, dwelling in our hearts with all His unsearchable riches.

(3) "The exceeding greatness of his power to us-ward who believe, according to the working of his mighty power, which he wrought in Christ, when he raised him from the dead." This power remains an enigma, a mystery, until the Holy Spirit reveals it by renewing us in the spirit of our mind to see, to desire, and to believe it.

These three great spiritual blessings summarize what a believer needs to know and needs the Holy Spirit to teach him. A sight, first of all, of all that God wants him to be. Then a consciousness of the wonderful riches and glory of this inheritance in His saints—nothing less than Christ in them. And then the living assurance that the almighty power of Christ's resurrection life is actually and unceasingly working in them to fit them for all that they are to be and to do for God.

How we need to believe in the glory of this mystery and in the power it would work in us. How we need to wait for the Spirit of divine wisdom to reveal it to us!

3. The lessons of this passage for those who are in the

ministry are simply invaluable.

They point to the three great spiritual blessings that summarize all that a Christian needs to know of what God has prepared for him.

They remind us that to preach these truths to believers is not sufficient; human wisdom cannot grasp them. If the knowledge is to be vital and effectual, it needs the illumination of the Holy Spirit to make us spiritual men. It is only the spiritual man who can discover spiritual things.

It is God himself, the Father of glory, who can and will give the Spirit of wisdom in answer to definite and persevering prayer.

It is the teacher, who has learned from the Spirit, and seeks to bring it home to others, on whom the duty rests of unceasing prayer that God would pour out the gift of the Spirit of wisdom on all to whom the teaching comes. Such teaching and such praying will lead believers to the full life which the epistle sets before them.

Let all ministers of the Gospel study and pray this prayer until every thought of preaching or teaching concerning the needs of individuals or of the Body of Christ is ever with the supplication, "Father of glory, give your children the Spirit of wisdom and divine revelation in the knowledge of yourself and all you have prepared to work in them."

CHAPTER TEN

1. *"That Christ may dwell in your hearts by faith."* In speaking of his conversion, Paul says, "It was the good pleasure of God to reveal his Son in me that I might preach him among the Gentiles." In our passage he tells us that this, his own experience, was the very sum and substance of his gospel. When he preached the unsearchable riches of

Christ, he preached Him as dwelling in the heart. He desired that none of his readers be without it. Without ceasing he pleaded with God to strengthen them with power in their whole inner life, that nothing would keep them from this wonderful blessing.

Many churches have lost the thought of Christ's indwelling being an experience for which Christians ought to seek. And yet how entirely Paul's teaching is in harmony with that of our blessed Lord. The night before His betrayal He spoke of the gift of the Holy Spirit: "At that day ye shall know that I am in my Father, and ye in me, and I in you." He then went on to add, "If a man love me, he will keep my word; and my Father will love him, and I will love him, and I will manifest myself unto him, and we will come unto him and make our abode with him." At the close of the High Priestly prayer, He asks, "That the love wherewith thou hast loved me may be in them, and I in them." It is evident that our Lord speaks here of something far beyond the initial grace of pardon and regeneration. He speaks of what would be given to those who love Him and keep His commandments; of something that would be the special gift of the Holy Ghost dwelling and working in them. Even so, Paul prayed that God would do something special and "mightily strengthen their inner man." Then, in his doxology he gives glory to God as able to do something "exceeding abundantly above all that we can ask or think." The blessing he holds out to us is that in which the spiritual life culminates as the highest exhibition of what the mighty power of God can work in us.

Christ dwelling in the heart. Let us begin where Paul begins, "I bow my knees." In urgent prayer for ourselves and for God's children around us, let us plead with God to do something according to the riches of His glory, which will lift us out of our feebleness and bring us into the life that will be to the praise of His glory.

2. The connection between being strengthened by the

Spirit and having Christ in the heart is brought out with great beauty in a sketch of the life of Miss E. Duncan in the book *The Christ-life* by Rev. J. B. Figgis. In a letter giving an account of her experience she writes: "I must write you to help me to magnify the Lord. He has been coming into my soul this past week as never before, and I am feeling most blessedly possessed with Him. For months the cry of my heart has been to be filled, and every week the longing grew more intense; not for joy—it was himself, himself, that is what I wanted. I had been longing and praying for this fullness of the Spirit, and yet I did ask the Lord to keep me waiting for a thorough preparation. He kept me waiting for months, but all that time I was waiting on the Lord and crying after the blessing with tears. Last Sunday evening the Holy Spirit came and has taken full possession. I do not know how to express my experience, for I seem to have lost all sense of experience in the sublime reality of His continual presence. When I could say I wanted neither happiness nor usefulness, but Jesus only, then the beloved Bridegroom came back, and I am perfectly satisfied with Him. I have God, and I want no more. Self has been subdued by the King reigning triumphantly. I see I have been erring and fancying I had a stock of grace within, instead of not only realizing that I am nothing, but also that I have nothing—that Jesus has it all for me."

In letters to friends she speaks of experiencing to the very depths the truths concerning the fullness of the Spirit. To one she writes: "Tell her not to rest until she is filled with the Spirit." To another, "Trust fully, follow fully, keep on trusting for the fullness of the blessing." To her fellow teachers, "May I give you a parting message: Be filled with the Spirit. Are you? Do you realize the tremendous blessing that will come to you, from you, if you are?"

In spite of the promise that the living water shall be in us springing up perpetually, many doubt the maintenance of such a life. But He who gave can keep. "One cannot live upon the mountaintops," a minister said to her. "I have lived upon them for months," she said. And those were months accompanied by suffering and agony. It would be easy to copy her absolute trust in God, but are we willing to climb? She was never weary of urging all she loved to seek to be filled with the Spirit, assured that His blessings were for them as much as for her. To one friend she sent the message: "God can satisfy her fully every moment; He has satisfied me for months with himself only." To another: "My earnest desire is that she may be filled with the Spirit, and then she will know what it is to be shut up to Christ." Elsewhere she says, "I used to pray: Lord, make me holy at all costs—with agony of body or mind if nothing else will do. And God took me at my word. I cannot tell you what joy it gives me that I consecrated all fully to the Lord. Tell every Christian it is worthwhile."

All this happiness was not for herself. Later, God allowed her to glimpse His view of the lost and to share some of His compassion for them. When cut off from pleading with others, she would plead for them before God—"plead all night if she had strength, and always with such certainty of being answered."

Perhaps the difference between being filled with the Spirit and not is seen most clearly when she says, "My besetting sin was pride: I know it was. Though I prayed to God for deliverance over and over again, I never got the mastery over it till I received the fullness of the Spirit. I did like praise, and you know I had plenty of it; but now when people praise me it does not seem to touch me—it falls off me like water off a dyke. I just feel I am sin—sin, nothing else, and every bit of good in me is all of God, and I want everyone to think so too."

This leads me to the last trait of character on which I would enlarge and stress. The presence that the grace manifested in her and the glory seen upon her were not hers, but given. In a deeply touching conversation, one of her doctors, speaking of the other, said, "Ah, he feels just as I do—not good, like you, but wicked." "Do you think me good?" "I do." "But I am not. We are just exactly alike—both poor sinners; but here lies the difference: what you see in me, and think good, is not me; it is not Emmeline Duncan, but the beautiful robe that Christ has put on me, and what you like is not me, but Christ, and He wants to clothe you with this robe too. Will you promise me to pray constantly: Reveal thyself to me, show me thyself? Just go into your room by yourself and speak to Him. He will save you; I know He will."

No wonder she could speak of the overwhelming sense of conscious union with Jesus.

CHAPTER SEVENTEEN

See *The Alps of the New Testament: A Study in Ephesians,* by Miss A. P. Ferguson. Huguenot College, Wellington (Maskew Miller, Cape Town).